Annoy Toy

Buoy Ahoy <u>Toy</u>

Overjoy Toy

& Toy

Hoi Polloi

Illinois Toy

Corduroy Toy

Employ Toy

Toy Toy.

Ed Fella '77

Table of C😐ntents

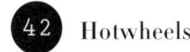
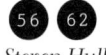

Publisher: Errant Bodies Press
Editor: Brandon LaBelle
Designer: Louise Sandhaus
Associate Editors: Matias Viegener, Giles Lane

We would like to thank the following organizations without whose continued support this issue of Errant Bodies would not have been possible: California Institute of the Arts and The California Arts Council*, a state agency. We would also like to thank Steve Lavine, Lynn Rosenfeld, Dick Hebdige, Ken Young, Darcy Huebler, CalArts Student Council and the Beyond Baroque Foundation.

Errant Bodies is planning a series of three books dedicated to Sound and Music, Design and Technology, and Architecture and Landscape. This series aims to address specific cultural practices in relation to the book as a form. Each book will grow from within the cultural practices it addresses, featuring works by those dedicated to its practice and evolution. The series will be published once a year beginning with "The Site of Sound: Of Architecture and The Ear" in the fall of 1998. These books, along with other Errant Bodies publications, are available through D.A.P. , Desert Moon Distribution and from the publisher.

Colophon: Fonts are *Bellvue*, Linotype Didot, **Folio**, and Prestige Elite. Cover type and special numbers designed by Ed Fella. Cover stock is CIS 12pt.; text stock is 70# Nekoosa Solutions in Blue Ice and Ivory. Printing by Foundation Press, Los Angeles

* any findings, opinions, or conclusions contained therein are not necessarily those of the California Arts Council.

my eyes are
peeled

| *by charlotte mew*

Life is too Short to be little Yourself.

I Overslept myself.

He bought a Dog.
The Dog died.
As Dogs do.

My father built me a House
but now he is Living in it Himself.

Miss Formica

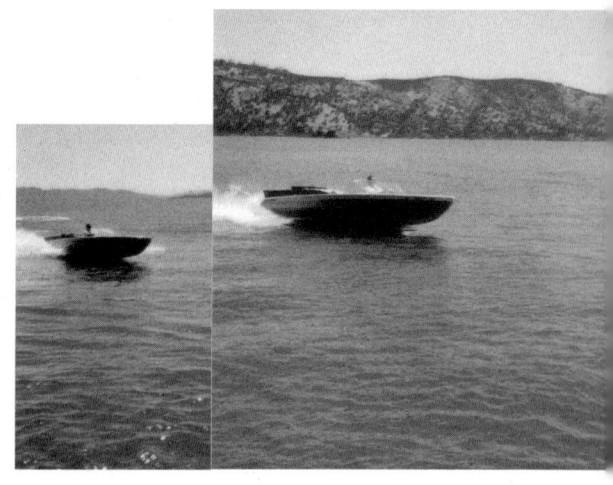

simon leung

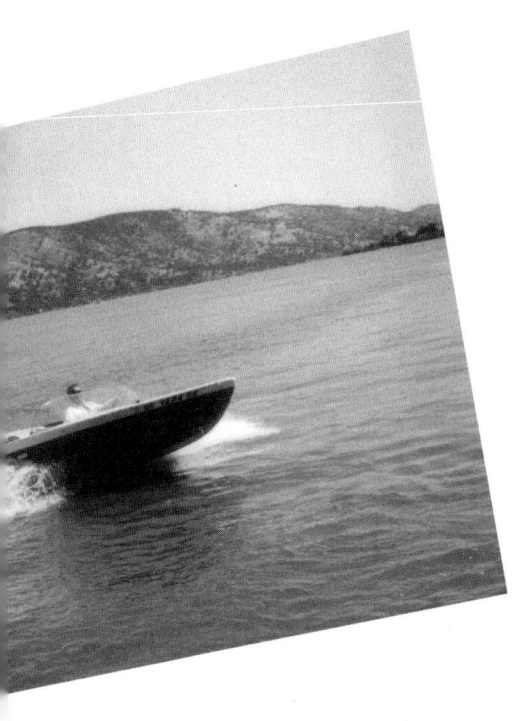

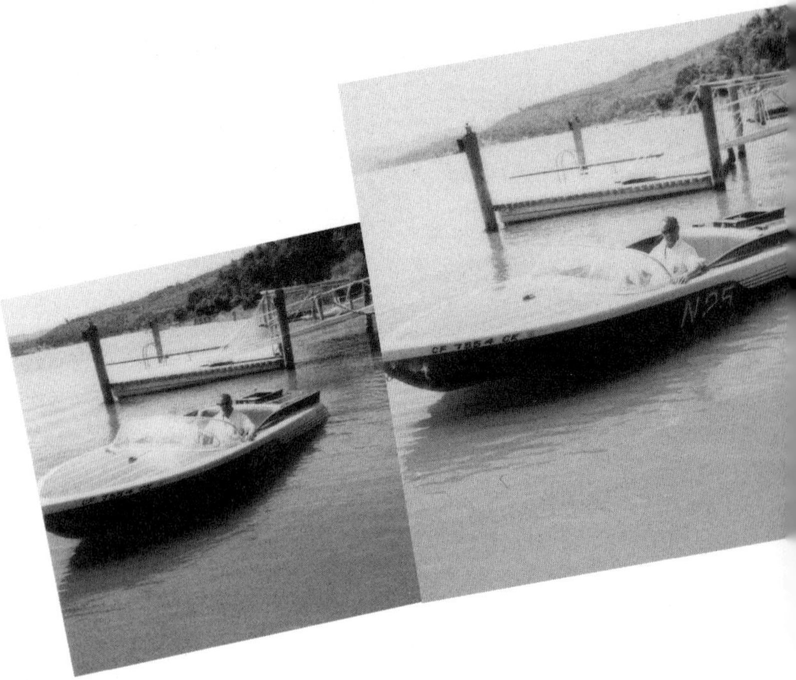

simon leung

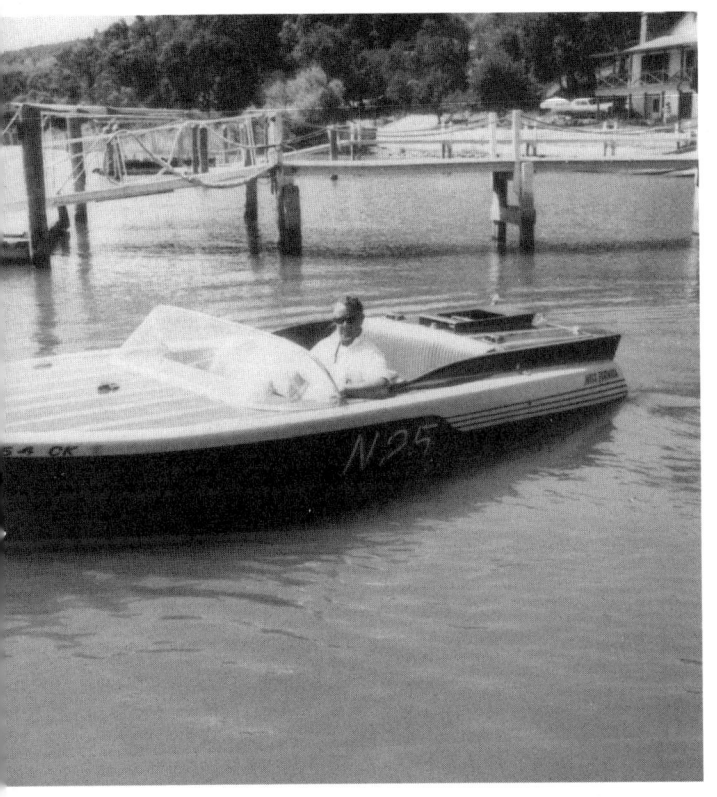

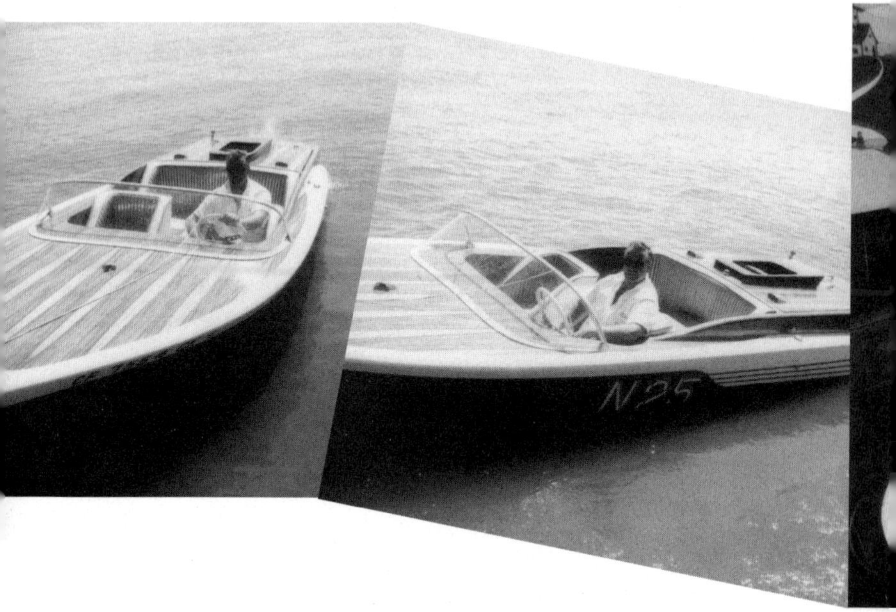

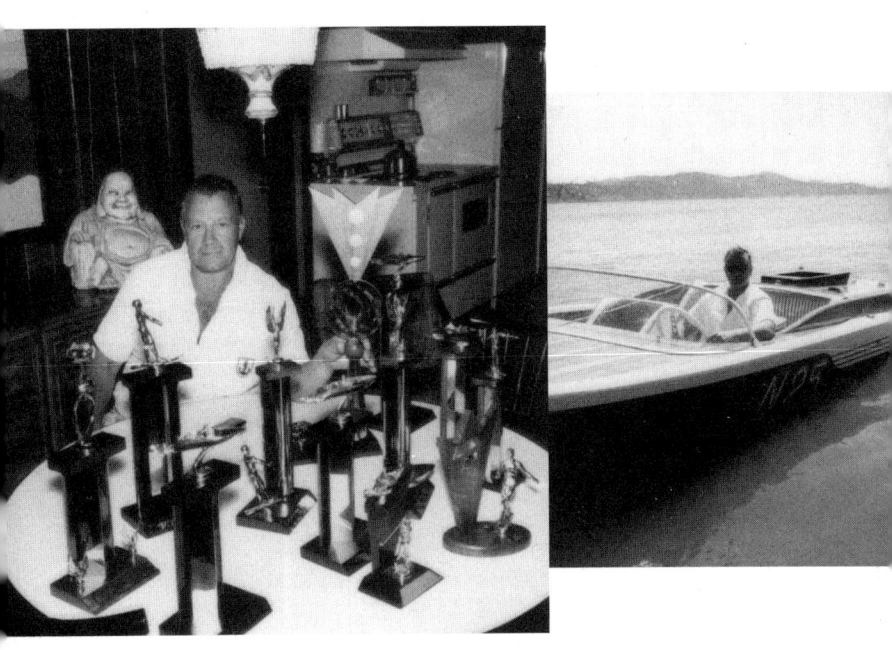

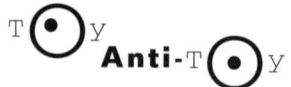

T(•)y Anti-T(•)y

| *by kitty scott*

It has been said that youth is no longer the domain of **the young and that North American culture is a playground for** infantile baby boomers and younger generations. Every playground needs play and toys. While play is a conscious part of my life, I have not been buying toys; however, at age 34, I have been given "playmobil"—a miniature toy world for children and, I suppose now adults. I have two ominous, yet diametrically opposed sets: one features a typical Canadian nature scene with prerequuisite moose, wolves, fir tree, and fern; the other belongs to the urbane world of media culture and consists of a French TV crew on a motorcycle and a directional road sign pointing to significant destinations. The team presumably shoots sports events such as the playmobil Tour de France, and evokes recent images of the French Paparazzi; one figure drives, while the other shoots with a hand-held video camera. Enchanted by this mass-produced playmobil "society," I have reluctantly become a toy collector.

I say "reluctant," because as an adult, I was certain my days of toy collecting were over. My passion for this tiny world, however, has collided with my professional practice as a curator and critic. Toys are re-occurring motifs in the artwork of two artists I have been studying of late. German artist Karin Geiger's photographs of teenage girls' bedrooms, as part of a larger project entitled *Inbetween* (1995-97), on occasion contain formidable plush toy collections. Artist Francis

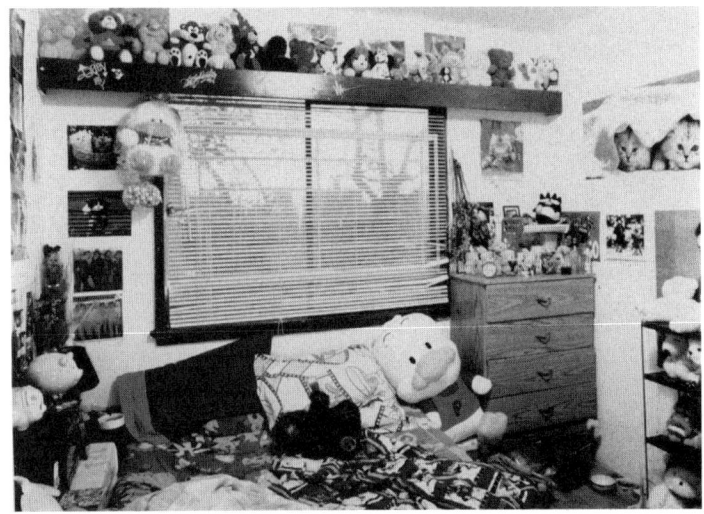

Alÿs's performance walks with magnetic toy dogs on wheels incorporate and make visible 'the play' embedded in all art practice. The artworks of Geiger and Alÿs are as different as my playmobil sets, yet they articulate the parameters of toys and the nature of play among two different generations and genders.

Geiger
photographs the world of adolescent girls. Leaving childhood and struggling towards adulthood, these girls reside in a liminal space where they are neither children nor adults. Still living at home, they are good girls, daughters and students, but they can also be lovers, mothers, smokers, users and runaways. By choosing to photograph these girls and the spaces they occupy, the artist represents a subculture rarely depicted in the field of contemporary art photography.

Geiger photographs these girls attending classes and hanging out. In their absence, she photographs

15

their school interiors and bedrooms. Not wanting to succumb to a single method of documentation, Geiger uses 35 mm, medium and large format, as well as the variety of photographic genres each format makes possible. She takes colour snapshots, individual and group portraits, black and white documents and interiors: some appear to be subjective, others ostensibly objective; some prints are small, others large.

While photographing the girls smoking together beyond the confines of the schoolyard, the artist got to know some of them and eventually gained access to the private world of their bedrooms. Geiger's intimate, but large-scale, documentary-style pictures of the girls' bedrooms depict their struggles towards adulthood. By pointing her camera into the corners of the rooms and including the ceiling within the frame, Geiger compresses the architecture and forces the display of their individual material lives.

While each room is a barometer of social class, education, leisure, mainstream consumption and sexuality, it is also always a treasure house holding an impressive and beautifully arranged collection of toys. In one photograph a long row of eternally happy plush beasts sit on the pelmet giving the effect of a Roman frieze. Felix the Cat and a big brown bear rest at the head of the bed. Tigger looks up adoringly from the floor. Beige bears, bunnies and a penguin are packed in on the top of the dresser. Stuffed white animals — Snoopy, assorted bears and others — fill a bookshelf in the foreground. Like the playmobil's human figures, all the plush toys smile submissively, as if to say, "buy me," and later "play with me."

Belgian artist
Francis Alÿs
's dogs are less a casualty of childhood, and more a con-

tinuation of its enduring impulses. His art
practice is centered around a core of walks
the artist has taken. Each stroll, document-
ed in photographs, is the consequence of an
idea. In the early 1990's while Alÿs was living in Mexico
and very much in the process of defining his language of
walks, he made, with the intent to produce an edition of
toys, a series of six little dogs to accompany him. Entitled
Collector (1991-92), each chunky chihuahua-sized pet is made of
rectangular pieces of magnetized iron and has four legs that
come to rest on small wheels. With the aid of a string, Alÿs walks,
or rather pulls the dog, throughout the city. The companion, no
doubt, eases the loneliness of solitary walking.

Obediently following his
master, the dog passively attracts
an outer coat consisting of metal
debris left on the streets and no

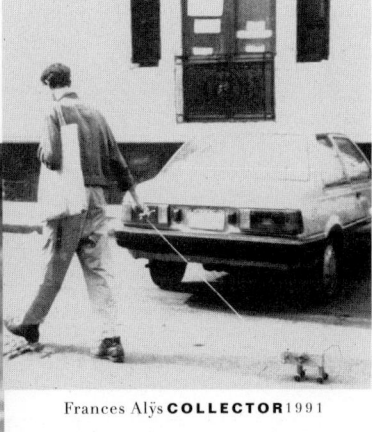

Frances Alÿs **COLLECTOR** 1991

longer desirable to anyone. Alÿs describes the walk: "For an inde-
terminate period of time, the magnetized collector takes a daily
walk through the streets and gradually builds up a coat made of
any metallic residue lying in its path. This process goes on until
the collector is entirely smothered by its trophies."

This action is a rendition of childhood play, casting the
performer as a child and the dog as toy companion. The dog—
sculpture and toy rolled into one—becomes ironically, less a
children's possession and more a sculpture the second it begins
to grow its new coat of rusted tin and old nails. Garbage is a for-
bidden plaything, presenting health risks to the young. In
contrast, the dog enters into the paradoxical history of valuable
art objects made with refuse. When the artist performs his walks,
one can speculate that he consciously inhabits a fantasy world
of play with the body and mind of an adult. By playing with his
"dog" in the city streets, the artist publicizes the necessity of play
in both art practice and the every day life of adults.

When taken together
these two different works of art extend the notion of what con-
stitutes a "toy" and the meaning of "play". The colorful assort-
ment of stuffed animals with wide eyes, turned-up mouths and
soft fabrics are the safe, yet highly sexualized objects of a child's
desires and subsequent gratifications. The toys are symptomatic
of the contradictions inherent in these girls' lives; while strain-
ing to be adults, the furry friends define the girls as partial
children. As toys, Alÿs's dogs somehow operate within the toy
economy, yet they are made of obsolete and potentially harmful
materials; they lack soft fur, happy faces, bright colors and the
surface quality of "newness." Alÿs's dogs are at once toys
and anti-toys.

Babes
in T●yland

by fred dewey |

A single tagline, from a two-page spread for a leather **jacket of unknown brand, announces "even a child can tell** you, there's no such thing as having too many toys." Illustrated by a young, pretty stud driving a sports car in a blur, the copy on the opposing page for the jacket speaks of "cars you'd sell your soul for." This little confusion, this little non-sequitur, does not put into the foreground the object being sold, but makes a much more visceral reference to something else. The product being sold is hinted at as an impossibility and thus, in the true American psyche, a necessity, as banally advertised as Warhol did with shampoo: we can have a glamorous life. You can, and also cannot, be an action figure, thus bound in the endless chains of signifiers that power permits. It is not only that the adult must have toys, but better, in this way you too can *signify*.

The complexity of effects between image and text in this revolutionary, avant-garde machinery of deposit and accumulation, of thematization, is stunning, encompassing our resistance to being sold to and our desire for it, for nothingness, to disappear to ourselves. It abolishes the links between us and objects in the world, those partial objects and their cogs and wheels, and asks us to join that realm where the world is killed, ungrounding us in the breakdown of our understanding and adherence to a new and ephemeral cult, that state where we are ready to buy anything. This little operation is meant to stun and undermine, however pathetic and pasty the argu-

19

ment one needs a toy as an adult, and that if one has this toy, one might then be hip. The fact few would consider selling their soul for a car doesn't matter; that we might does. The old proposition, that old, ultra-Reaganesque death march, that "the person who dies with the most toys wins," is a reversal of the social fact that the person who toys with the most death becomes a hero of the revolution. Now such reversals of actuality have become ubiquitous, the foundation of the violence which masquerades as power. Out of such decimations whole stretches of the American mind have been turned into lifeless deserts and lagoons.

"Toys, toys, more toys," said Michael Dertuzos, appositely of the computer science lab at MIT. This great avant-garde processing is not technically but politically cybernetic. Roy Disney, vice chair of Disney's board, speaking of their empire noted that Uncle Walt would have found "the size of it" "amazing." "Disneyland will always be special because it was the first. There's a nostalgic quality. You feel like you are in a toy world and there's always something interesting around the next corner."

Where Babies Come From

In 1902, at the dawn of an America premised on the ruination of localism and the ubiquity of great, centralized processing networks, Children's Day was started at the Marshall Fields department store in the midwest. It was based on a banal and farfetched idea: "children are future customers." Pure science, and pure fiction, toys and future would be welded to the machining of probability. Commercialism, a ravenous, mutating alien, was reviled throughout America; unable to manage the fractious, uncooperative people, pragmatism struck upon a technique and non-place it could manage the people into. Sidonie Gruenberg, a progressive authority on "child care," formulated in 1912 the device: a separate children's world.

We must not call children good or bad; to
be progressive meant to see children as
things to be channeled and rationalized.
Field's advertisers chimed in: we stand, they
said, before "the vast unfolding of the modern child-
world." Was this new continent to teach the tools of
citizenship, preparing youngsters for the tough business
of political adulthood? No. It was, for Fields, a territory "impor-
tant to this mercantile institution."

By 1926, while in Europe most toys and clothes were
still made at home, in avant-garde America, play-things were
mass produced. By 1928 the social machine had turned things
upside down and inside out; a whole magazine was already devot-
ed to and called *Toyworld*, stating in an immeasurably complex
series of oxymorons "play is the child's business; toys the material with which he works." This new business was no longer any
of an adult's business: this world within the world must develop
on its own. We are familiar with the traditionally communist and
party bureaucratic uses of youth. But few have examined how, as
business changed into empire and mercantilism, these in turn
invented and mastered techniques with similarly fictional and
devastating results. Mercantilism was bound up with pragmatism, in some ways its clearest realization: learning by doing.
Parents had to buy for their children because spending was
respect for a new world unto itself. While we still barely know
how this virus could propagate, mechanisms of collectivization
were key. The republic, in spite of party myths, generally had little taste for racism. Yet somehow the first true mass market toy
between 1915-17 was the Alabama Coon Jigger, a mechanical,
laughing, prancing Negro avatar sold in Wanamaker's
and elsewhere. Here, as in cinema with *Birth of a Nation*,
an early mass organizing operation appearing as culture

played to the most base and terrified of American sensibilities.

Why the use of the African-American, at this time already thoroughly reconquered and, first and most viciously with the rest of the population, reduced to laboring for survival? What the Coon Jigger suggests is that the separate world of children was linked, through humor, with the tragedy of labor, once unacceptable for most Americans as a sign of machinism and slavery: the black represented this horror, ridiculous and without glamour, a nightmare in need of purging. Children were being drafted as agents in collective privatization, new members of a universal ghetto created by mercantilism, toys one substrate through which this nasty business could be achieved. Here indeed were the first ways of entertaining oneself to death. Though a separate world of children was in this way carved out of the public realm for conquest, the creation of a mass society through children required compulsory laws pulling children out of the work force for intensive training or political death at an early age. Unfortunately, the business of America had been turned into business, or as psychologists and economists would say, development.

The Principle and the Pauper

Mass society achieved the transformation of the marvelous into the banal on a colossal scale; now, so many years later, toys have become immeasurably serious, part of an arsenal of psychological and worldly warfare waged against the political from birth. Play has ceased to bear upon self-government, thinking, and acting, and has become fantasizing in elaborate, pre-made narrative conditions. We are already at a point where toys have nothing to do with the world, as they did even in my childhood, but with the fantastic narratives spun out through media channels and conduits. Children are taught to separate

22

from their parents and join this new world,
learning to make decisions based on what
is playing out on screens around them. The
Coon Jigger turned into the Buck Rogers
pistol, and from there to Barbie, The Jetsons, and He
Man. The participation in clichés begins early, as children interact with fictions that have achieved an unprece-
dented social penetration. This disposition to fantasy through
the toy is very different from imagination, from a relation to partial objects that helps the child make a transition to the world.
The corruption at issue is that the toy-like in principle is a fundamental aspect of learning to envision and imagine one's world,
going back to the objects ancient Greeks used to vote with called
ballots, a tiny, toy-like disk on an axle; it fit in a slot, ran down a
chute, and through this, large numbers of people learned to manage things. The toy-like in principle embodies preparation for
exercise of capacities, primarily because acting freely in the world
is no child's game, obedience no virtue. We are not in the nursery any more.

In some sense, what we face is a new world where we
can exist as adults in name only, which is to say, as biological and
social creatures, but not political; the separate world has grown
and spread to consume the republic, the mercantile fiction a total
phenomenon. The rise of toys as partial objects which refer to
fictions and mass media rather than mastery in the world, dimin-
ishes the disappointment that comes in the world precisely
through the limitations of toys, their transitionality; now, because
the fictions extend everywhere, toys never truly end; with the
breakdown of one, a new one can be bought. The limits of fantasy appear less and less. Adulthood is about overcoming
such disappointments, the powerlessness of childhood,
to imagine oneself into the actual world as a complex,

rich, non-commercial, non-laboring activity, as making. But as the whole world becomes toyworld, the opportunities for such education, and hence adulthood, diminish. The site of labor, as brutal and murderous as it is, is actually the sandbox of power, while the real violence is exacted in a political realm we can no longer know or grasp. By never allowing us to experience the disappointment of a world we cannot control, and so must seek to govern on our own, toyworld blocks political adulthood. What is the pop icon but a toy? What are people but toys relentlessly toyed with? What is our culture now but an impossibility because of toyworld?

The Price Versus the Priceless

Toyworld's foremost aim is to eliminate all understanding of culture — in distinction to the fiction of culture spread by a mercantile mass society — as the activity of helping us manage the difficult world after the nursery, so adults can imagine richly in ways that are not childish, at the same time preserving toys and their marvels for childhood, where they belong. Toys are the rightful realm of child play, freedom the rightful realm of adult play. Expanding toyworld to overwhelm adulthood abolishes the appearance of politics, its overt existence. We are thus left to face the merchandising, and so disappearance, of every moment in life, producing a thematization or fictionalization of the world. The theme park, the totalism of the toy as toyworld, is merely one example of the model for how this can be done, but really it is any metaphysical envelope, *a world within the world*, believing we must enter an environment that belongs to someone else in order to imagine, think, act, and be. That this fictional nursery could be presented as a realm without friction, divergence, or mess, as even a real nursery can never be, is the essence of the virtualism. The virtual surpasses friction, which

is infantilization; discovery of its insuffi-
ciency, and revelation of friction as the
great educator is rather than the beginning
of education, a blow saved for us until the
very end. As the hypertrophy of mass society, virtualism
spreads, the nesting of separate worlds within worlds,
fictions and impossibilities seen only as necessities.
Biologically and socially mature, we remain childlike when it
comes to the facts of power, hoping not to know them, to regress
into a state where all is taken care of. Toyworld means glamour,
a wonderful action story with us moving through the deserts and
lagoons of a rented existence.

Once inside the empire of toyworld, the first glimpse of
adulthood children get in the toy that breaks down, disappoints,
that is limited, slips away. Just as childhood teaches through the
limitation of toys and their ability to signify infinitely even when
limited, in the infinite fictions of commercial mass society and
the perpetual purchasing of the new, this education, perhaps the
greatest gift of toys, is eliminated. As toys become more complex
and mass produced their context becomes more and more pre-
determined, a world made by and for others. Action is thereby
regulated and limited, replaced with "interactivity". Now we have
a toy sixteen inches tall that can move its arms and legs, croon
17 songs, play games like peek-a-boo, costs $100, and for $65
more links with TV episodes and videos. Interactivity is the totalism of toyworld, the next frontier. The cyberpet, a computer chip
which uses its clock to signal when it requires "care," needs to
be "fed," "get medicine," or be "cleaned-up after," has been
absurdly described as the "marriage of technology and the 20th
century version of hugging." Clearly, there is a relishing
of the elaborate, pre-set fiction, of total meaninglessness
in the navigation of complex fabricated objects bound

into networks; deliberately distant is the affirmation of the capacity to play and imagine with easily obtainable and often free things like a match, a sheet, a bottle cap, or a porch overhang.

The most necessary target for elimination in children is the discovery that imagination arises first and best easily, at no cost, out of nothing. To learn this is to begin to be free. It is not hard to remember days when I would find within a box of four or five wood block shapes the means to build whole cities, and even inhabit them, for days on end. So with a simple stream, building dams out of leaves, twigs and sand, my hands covered with cold water and dirt, messing around until dinner, finding in this a rise and fall of the ineffable that corresponded in no way to anything that had been or would be, yet to all of these. The best moments of my childhood were always around things I could arrange and rearrange infinitely as basic objects, even fabricated things like miniature logs for log cabins, pieces of interlocking plastic to build, a set of couch cushions, a Superman cape donned to jump off the back of chairs and stair landings. What might I be, what could I do? The idea was not to banally repeat what was offered me, but to make things more interestingly. Toys taught inadvertently the miracle of one's own free powers and the freedom of the world.

Toying With Life

What then is a toy, and what is politics? When everything is an artifact, everything intersects in the omnipresence of toys rather than in leaving toys behind. Things and people, unloosed from everything, float in a great motion, as the screen we wield against ourselves and others wraps neutralizing envelopes of fantasy into an invisible harness. Toys do not come to life and help, wooden soldiers marching to our rescue. Children are unique in believing this might occur; political children believe this will occur. We buy into things as if they were toys, expecting they will solve our problems, expecting them to revive an imagination burned out at the roots. The commodity and toy are part of this simulacra, hiding fictions behind fictions, wheels within wheels, to manufacture the final story that we could be toys and commodities, that this total meaninglessness could be an imagination and a culture.

The movement of this is "that distinguished thing" Henry James called death, constructed against the imagination, making the world slip from our grasp every morning when we wake up. Toy and spectacle, like economics and technology, are the unmoved movers. How did such an organizing fiction-movement overthrow our common world? What is it that is disappeared when we are? Toys encourage early bonding in mass society and its total fiction; fitting into pre-existing collectivized structures, disguised as business and merchandising, becomes the point at which children are trained, not as a doorway to the unlimited world but as a lock against actualization, against even sensing the world. And so the inner child creates the inner adult, the adult who lives in exile from him or herself and can have no externality, no appearance. Adults are trained to imagine at every point in preset ways made for them, via the mass-manufactured and mass-disseminated, but most of all through their own nothingness. The capacity to inhabit the virtual is carried forward from an obliterated childhood, the surplus at the top of the ledger carried into the next column of adulthood, leaving us groundless. Trained as consumers of manufac- tured fiction, our incapacity to imagine is extended infinitely in and through objects in the world, creating a dead end inside the world. Nothing is actual in the little theater. The levers and gears are controlled by those who play with bigger toys than you and you aren't allowed in their playpen. The tragedy is that those playing no longer know what they are playing with.

The Nothingness of Toying

Walking to work one day, having gone a couple miles and ending up on a familiar yet unfamiliar sidestreet — my car had been towed for parking in a driveway — I passed a yard. Behind a chain link fence were dirty, plastic colored toys lying around, beat-up, forgotten colored plastic shapes for climbing, the residue of some past joy abandoned. There were no kids, and somehow it seemed they had been gone for some time, leaving behind the broken pieces, hoolahoops, a choo-choo, in piles, refuse. What was so scary about these abandoned, dirty, broken toys left outside, as they so often are, in a back yard? Suddenly the banal fantasies of childhood were apparent, making me nauseous. The wonder that toys represent is the infinite capacity to imagine, yet the reality is perhaps not so pleasant. Fantasy is insufficient, its instruments limited, its results non-existent; once the children are gone we come face to face with truth. Baudelaire spoke of taking toys apart to deform them, breaking them down into fragments only to find there is no soul. Why then build the world back up out of such things? Does one build something because one imagines in the world, or because one is playing with the world as a toy? Why build a model, a simulation, a toy, a theory? In the course of existence, we are born, bringing a new vantage into the world, advancing from childhood to adulthood, doing what we can against the odds. Society bears down, and yet, to say we are political children is to say we know little of that realm that can protect that unique vantage. After a century of mass society there seems to be no space to

28

prevent us from becoming toys, playthings of our own automatisms and those of others, of the technology and violence which calls itself power but is the rule of no one. We play with the very processes of life, of time, of space, the structures of life, the future of humanity, as if they were games and things. This is the horror born of political children, a horror whose mindlessness threatens the existence of the world and every last living thing.

When there are no political adults left, when all power has been devoured and turned into violence, who is left to educate the children, to teach them of the world and their capacity for freedom in it? Who and what any more can teach us what it is to imagine in the world, to act and be adults in every way? This is the question every person, leaving the comforts of the nursery behind, faces on the doorstep of a world where toys are useless.

Sources:

Gant ad [NYT 11/97]; Disney quote [LAT 7/16/95]; historical [William Leach, *Land of Desire*, 86-7, 328, 86]; Cyberpets [NYT 11/6/97]

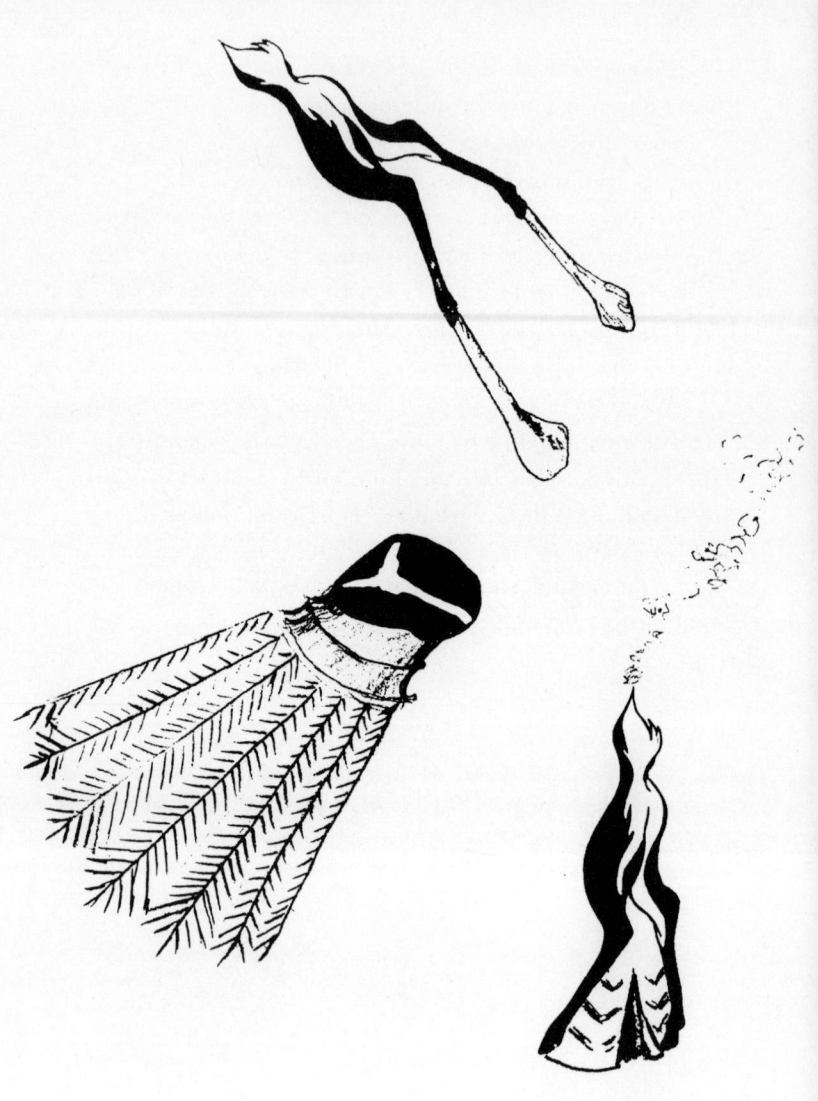

karen dunbar

30

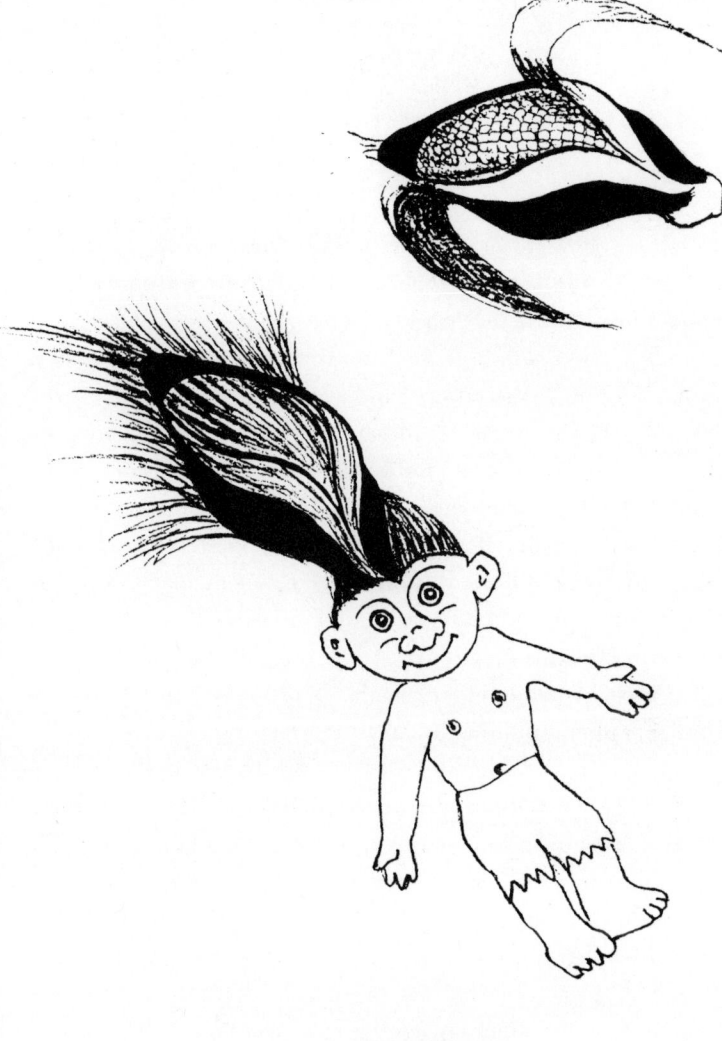

Bambi butt wishbone
Bambi ear of corn
Bambi ear troll
Bambi butt teepee
Bambi nose shuttlecock

Vari●us Gray Waves (1 and 3, 2 and 4)

| *by carol & elizabeth treadwell*

1.   They never actually played. They got up, maybe ate, **scorned any thought of switching out of their pajamas. Mold** could form for all they cared.

Their round people*and their round people's houses, cars, buildings: these were fundamental.

The wooden round people with their plastic hair and heads. Their incomplete towns: a school and a parking garage, but no bank or supermarket.

The sisters fought over certain people. A certain taller girl — they agreed she was not quite a woman, maybe a teenager — blue painted body and blonde plastic ponytail. She was desired. She was fought over. There was only one of her.

The bodies of the people not just symmetrical but cylindrical, radial: spinning them left no trace, no ghost of color.

All morning, sweat gathering behind their knees or between their toes and fingers, the two sisters involved themselves in setting up. In the spreading out of the town. The determination of its angle in relation to the walls, the stairs, their father's feet. The choice between a dense, urban configuration and a scattered, rural one.

"I want my family to live way down a road."

"Fine, I want my family far from yours, anyway."

Distressed: "But maybe they can still ride bikes over?"

"Maybe."

Stomachs flattening the breath out of them.

32

And Mom would drift by:

"Haven't you girls started playing yet?"

The smell of fat cooking might waft by, ignored.

The round people all lined up along the border of the town. All in a line, waiting to be chosen.

They had three little brown-haired girls in red dresses: two newish and one weather-beaten. Thinned paint showing the wood underneath. Some of the newest ones were made of all plastic. Of these they were skeptics.

Finally the selection of families would occur.

It'd take fingernails dug into the pearly undersides of forearms and heels shoved hard and repeatedly into inner thighs to do it. Slaps on shoulders. Screams just under parental audibility before the auction came to its conclusion.

The boy with the red pot slammed over his head like a cap was always left over, often thrown fast at a face or a stomach.

"Hah, hah, you take him!"

And thrown back.

"No! You get him!"

And thrown again, let to slam into a far wall, hopefully under a chair or radiator. The handle of his pot long since broken off.

(He and his fellow motleys often becoming a "dead family" or an orphanage.)

Then the creeping smiles. After the kids had been assigned the best bedrooms. The blonde pony-tailed girl getting the best one of all. Getting the master bedroom. After it was determined that the adults would sleep in their driveways, upright in their cars.

The creeping smiles and the already-answered question: "You don't still want to play or do you?"

33

There was, clearly, nothing more to do with these things now.

2 .   We will make these little wooden people with round plastic heads swim in the edges of foam. Later, be in Rome, say, hey I want that one prize.

They live on the edges of sand castles and rivers in mud like brown sugar. Our underwear rides up and our shorts are wet. Or we have Wonder Woman bathing suits and singsong "tough titty said the kitty when the milk was gone."

Recently I visited my younger cousin Tracy who, between our Dr. Mario Olympic events with Mike and April, shyly showed me her bucket of little plastic people with round plastic heads. My enthusiasm may have taken her by surprise, but she got on her face one of those inside out smiles you don't quite want to be showing. We lined them up on a lightly polished half wall that is made of wood to separate the dining room from the living. Though now that Tracy's family has moved in and now that our grandma has died it seems almost to be made of the same fabric as our grandma's body.

My uncle, Tracy's pop, showed us her rings on his return from the hospital. Only ever before had they lain amidst ashtray and novel on her beside table.

Tracy was kind enough to line up her people for a photo. We sorted them by color of clothes and hair. There were several sets of triplets. I angled for her to make a gift of one to me, but she held her ground quite firmly (Tracy wants to be a policewoman after her football—oriented career).

I mentioned that it had always seemed strange to me that the lady-round-people had curves that went all the way around both on top and bottom. Elizabeth said, "how come the moms' tits go all the way around their bodies?"

3 .   Play promises.

Knock your sister down on her back.

Straddle her.

(No, her head does not crack on the floor.

Her neck tenses, lowers it incrementally.)

Pin her hands back, palms to palms.

Fingers like crab legs.

Stare. She'll stare.

Let the saliva bubble between your lips. In a thin line, pulsing.

She may now notice the ceiling above you.

Scream.

Make her promise.

Her knees cocked behind you. Can't reach to kick.

It doesn't matter what she promises.

She'll promise more before you let her up.

Make her promise never to call you by your name.

Keep her hands down. Every knuckle.

"I promise, I promise."

"Never?"

She may resist now. Knowing she can't keep it.

You may need to slam up and down. Crash down on her stom-ach.

It doesn't matter what she promises.

She'll promise anything you ask.

You'll be mad with power, omnipotent.

Above defiance, above crafting penalties.

When you let her: she'll be loose-eyed, panting, slow to get up.

You'll be loose-limbed and slappable.

You'll stand next to each other.

Pretending the roles are permanent.

4.   *"a muffled sound between X and now*
          where swollen bodies have been stacked like logs"

                                    — Michael Palmer

In research we went to Kmart. The round people have become more rotund. They've flattened, somehow — there's been a shift in perspective. I couldn't believe it, our hands had grasped perfectly. The black ones have more "realistic" hair now. Methods of Barbie beget each other. And there is a little pink cellular with round rainbow buttons and a little blue with square. Look though, still barely mutated, is the old fashioned rotary on a string. Let's see, and a fancy night light for infant rock shows on the ceiling. Go to sleep, go to sleep.

After Margaret was born, Carol and I tried to fall asleep with our arms curled up grabbing the air as she did. It never, of course, worked, and as I woke, slow or quick, to find my arms helpless as Lincoln Logs on the bed beside me, I felt an awful lot like Mr Floppy Armed Bert on "Sesame Street." Perhaps that is still why I prefer a striped shirt above all other items of clothing.

At Kmart I bought: a light for my bike, film for my camera, a pack of cigs, and some birth control.

Carol and I had a third game. As you come home in the backseat from supermarket or school, look about you, these apartments you live in are dominoes, set precariously atop each other. And you are the ants who reside there. The way the curb meets the street can't help but remind you of the yellow edge of that plastic house meeting the carpet, or your other poor metal dollhouse which was sat on and severely dented by a boy you didn't even want to invite to your party.

* "round people": a FisherPrice product elsewhere referred to as "little people" or "village people"

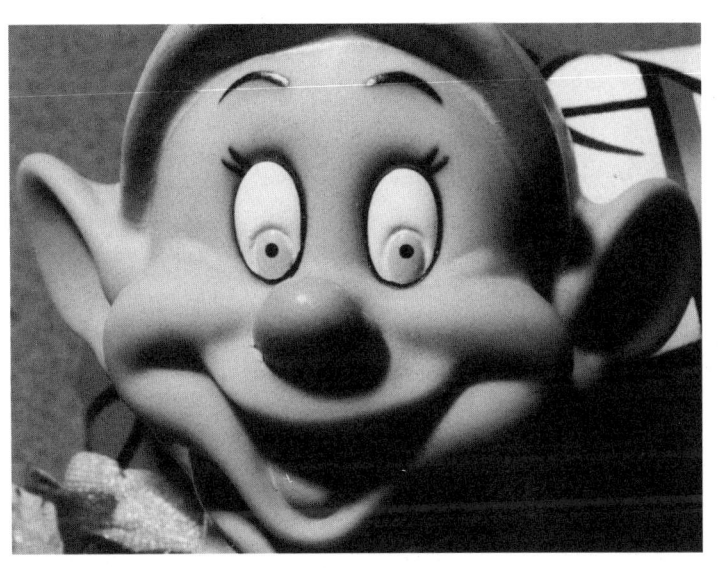

steven hull

Jonas Eggen

Krusesgt 9, 0263 Oslo, Norway.

Dear Brandon,

Human kind is huddling towards winter 97 and as you can see, I have not been able to put anything down on paper for the next issue of Errant Bodies. I am a dyslexic Norwegian who likes to write, and would in particular have liked to write for the next issue on toys. But as I have not been able to get a life after my studies, I am at the moment still living in a collection of cardboard boxes and heavy trunks, and my writing difficulties makes it very problematic for me to produce any text without a substantial amount of space and time. Therefore I am sending you only this note of regret.

Regarding what I would have liked to write about, I could for the sake of it mention some topics:

Something based on C.G. Jung's notion that people in Western, contemporary societies, are not capable of becoming adults, maybe in a similar way to domestic cats and dogs. For example a Scottish dollhouse shop which denies children access, or Martin Margiela´s real- size Barbie clothes. Also, N. Postman's entertained citizens.- Electronic pets or bungie jumping. And the notion of the playing human (Homo Ludens), to suggest that there is nothing new under the sun.

About a Danish survey proving that crap toys produce a generation of wasters, with a lack of respect for objects/products, as well as the environment, and no faith in repair or maintenance.

About children, who by their politically correct parents, are prevented from watching Transformers and similar toy promoting cartoons, and that the consequence of this lack of information, and initiation to contemporary TV culture, is actually a form of exclusion from the play ground and causes isolation. " No No! Ostrich Man don't lay eggs with the Quantum Mice, neutron brain!!" This could be discussed in relation to children elsewhere, where play is an imitation of, and thereby an initiation to parental activities.

I would have liked to have written something about the arts, in which artists and I, use and make Toys or toy-like things. Something about how these artworks function upon the public, adults as well as children, and how these works, as with toys themselves, often are gifts. Interpretations of these relationships - art toys and gifts, and eventualy something about Lewis Hyde, the author of "The Gift", and his notion about the relationship between the words "Gift and "gifted".

A toy, or an artwork relating to toys, when a gift, can serve as a licence to creativity and the imagination, both for receiver and giver. Is it therefore possible, that when your dad buys you a model train set, or a Sony playstation, he's not only buying this for himself, but is buying access to your world?
-This could be compared to Virginia Axline´s "Dib´s World", where she, as a therapist, gets to know and help a little boy through play with toys.

Contemporary play with toys could be interpreted as a reference to more surreal, or at least virtual narratives and realities, in opposition to the rational and reality confronting ones (which at least here in Scandinavia were so strongly encouraged during the 60´s and the 70´s). If you watch the earlier mentioned contemporary cartoons, you easily get the feeling that the authors must be on some seriously mind altering drugs. Except for the difficulties in finding the plot, it can also be extremely hard to understand or find the morals and other, until now, necessary educational components of a story. The discrepancy between realities becomes in this, and the following situation, very interesting.

Because, finally, I would have liked to compare this contemporary play with toys, to the phenomenon of cargo cult. As when "The Gods"/western entrepreneurs, first paid certain Pacific people a visit, and their colonial activities: "UFOs and landing pads", casually performed "funny-liquid rituals around altars while reciting magical spells", were actively imitated and copied in wood and clay by the aborigines. But after a short period, where one would have observed something that looked like a primitive theme park, or a contemporary kinder garden, the "Gods" departure and the absence of desired effects from the new found rituals, brought the abandoned islanders down in desolation and decay.

But as they say somewhere; "To late is always to late", And I can therefore only say that I would be very happy to contribute to ´Errant Bodies´ in the future. Perhaps I am a dilettante or to use the more flattering term genealogist, meaning that I have an interest in everything, and as a dyslexic, I naturally can connect anything to anything, so please let me know of any future topics for the journal. (Maybe books ?)

Thank You so much for the letter, the invitation, your faith, and not to leave unmentioned how the following sentence flattered me; "I was given your name by a friend of mine who saw your work..."

Thank you for Your Persistence!

Yours sincerely, Jonas Eggen

Iv never caled over-
Sea's before, - better
Conection than to Danmark...

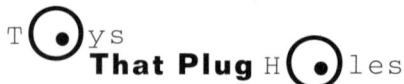

Toys That Plug Holes

| by alden smith

and so there are holes
in me that are not static
they move
swelling in the colder months
with hours short on daylight

holes diminished even if only a little
at the age of four or six or eight
at the sight of some new brightly colored thing
finely wrapped and given warmly
by an aunt or a godmother or the neighbor kid
with the large lips

holes narrowing at age twenty four
under the occasionally covetous glances
of Japanese girls with skin of an
almost unbearable whiteness
smelling of chestnuts and damp river grasses

vacancies occasionally diminishing
as my palms move
across my wife's almond skin
as she softens under
a touch still awkward after seven years

and so there are vacancies in me
that without reprieve
will remain open
and moving
occasionally speaking at me

like that stuffed bear tossed without thought
into the basket
in the corner of the room where even now
I would not go of my own volition

Hotwheels

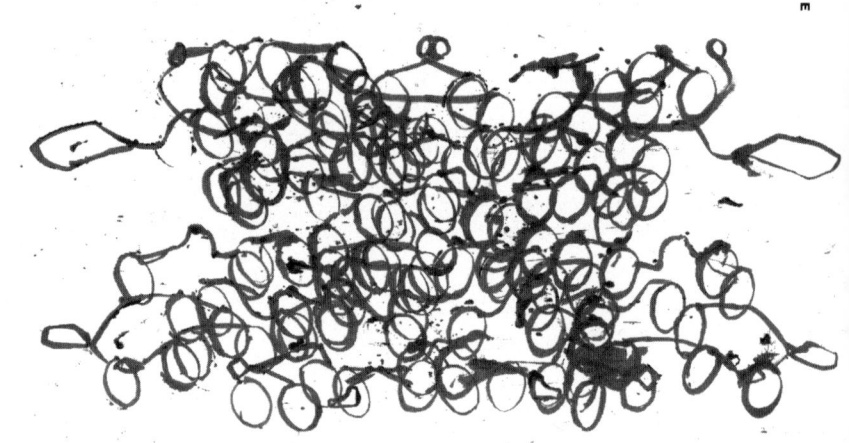

steve roden

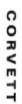

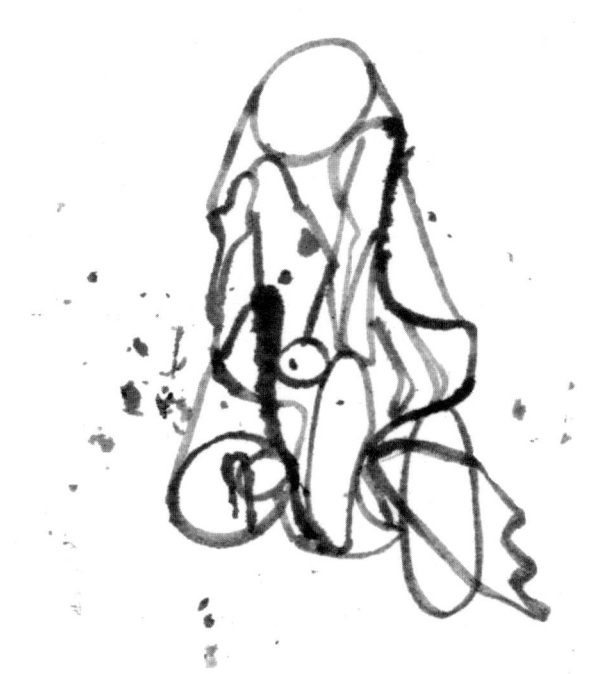

43

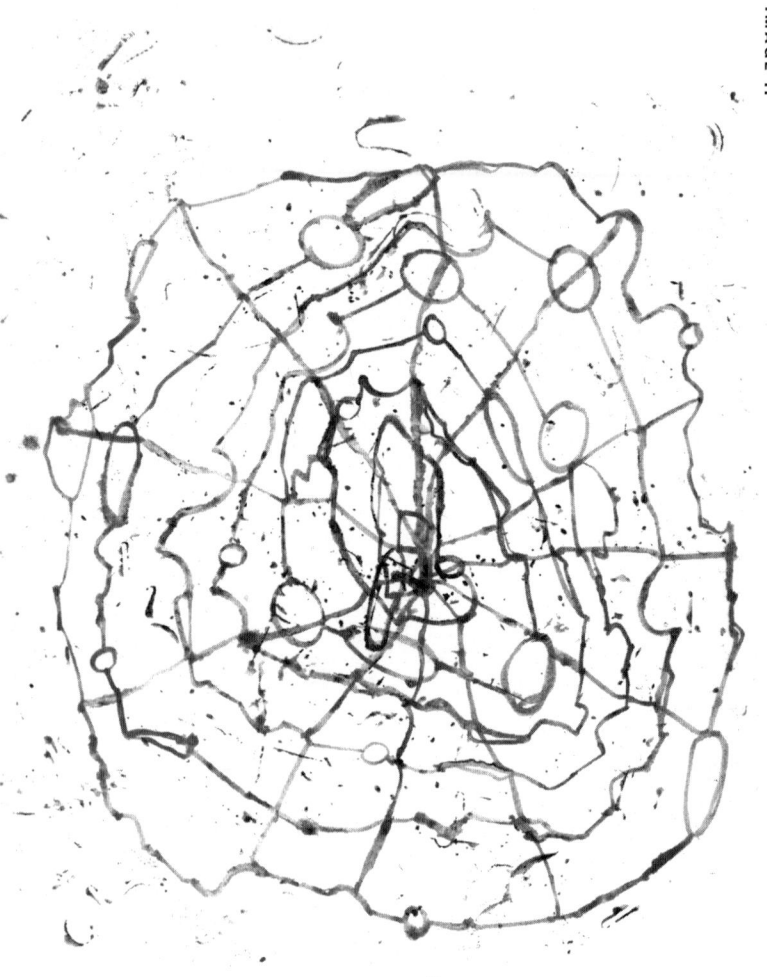

steve roden

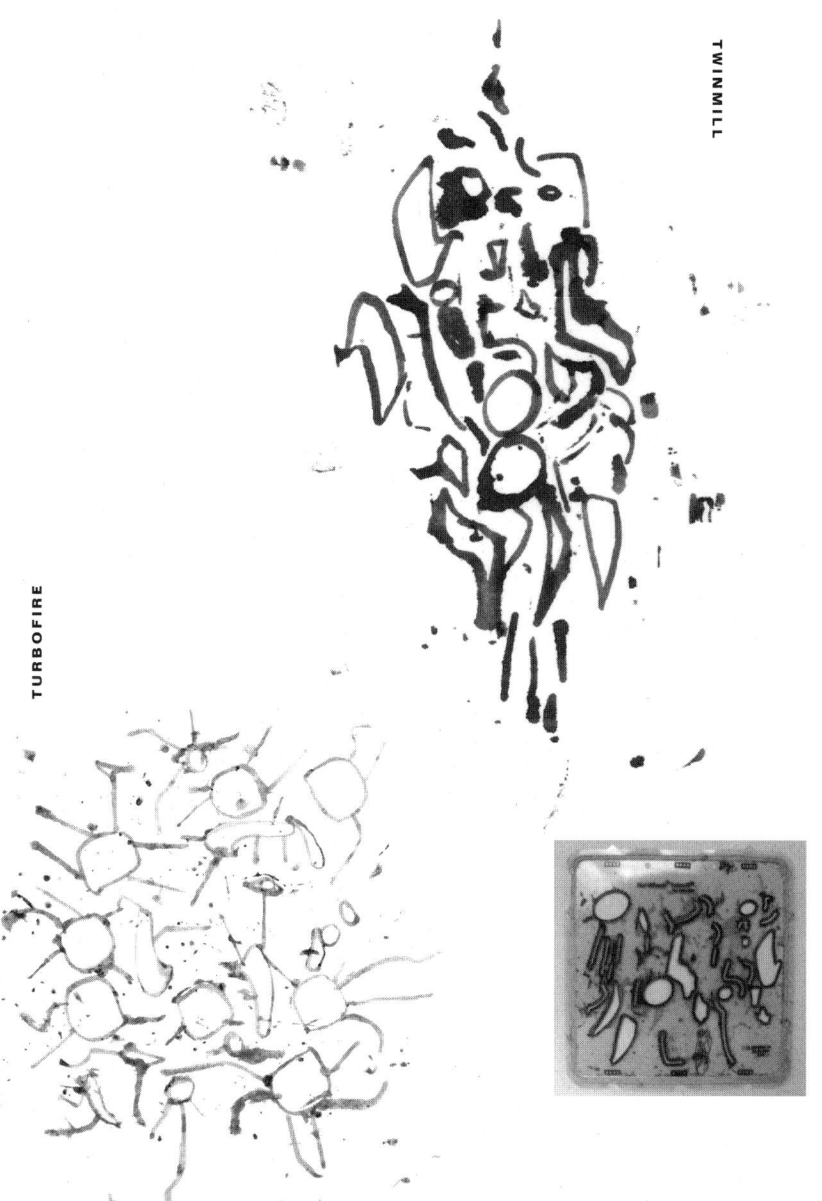

TWINMILL

TURBOFIRE

Riding Red 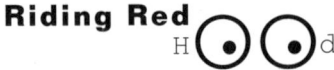H ● ● d

| by theresia rosa kleeman

My Aunt Eugenie sent a gift for my tenth birthday. I open-

ed the present's wrapping to find a long rectangular box with

transparent cellophane inserted in the lid. Through this window

violet   I could see her looking at me. Her beauteous blue eyes and cher-

ry stained lips begged me to open the box. To release her I

untwisted the wires around her throat and waist; then lifted her

from her container. A small booklet fell out from under her skirt.

lavender   In gilded letters it read "Little Red Riding Hood: A Classic
silver
glaciers   Madame De Saint-Ange Doll." Her sunny yellow braids and soft

ringlets around her brow were topped by a tall pointed conical

eye   hood complete with cape cascading down from the nape of it:

the reddest of fabrics imaginable. I thought it a certainty that this

blues   red hooded cape could make her fly as though she were a cardi-

nal bird. I wanted to fly with her on fantastic adventures.

"We will be great friends!" I said to her as I wrapped her

little arms around my neck and squeezed so firmly I thought I

heard a tiny "Owie" extend from her soft felt lips.

pools   Like cherries indeed, the luscious slope of these curves

asked to be bit. To be bit hard causing overly ripe juice to squirt

out and drool down my chin. I did not bite her then, not quite

yet. She smelled new and untainted. In a doll's life this state of

things does not last very long. She would fray and stink from the

daily abuse of a filthy pre-pubescent child. I knew this

and wanted to enjoy her seductive freshness at least

until the candles were blown out and the last piece of

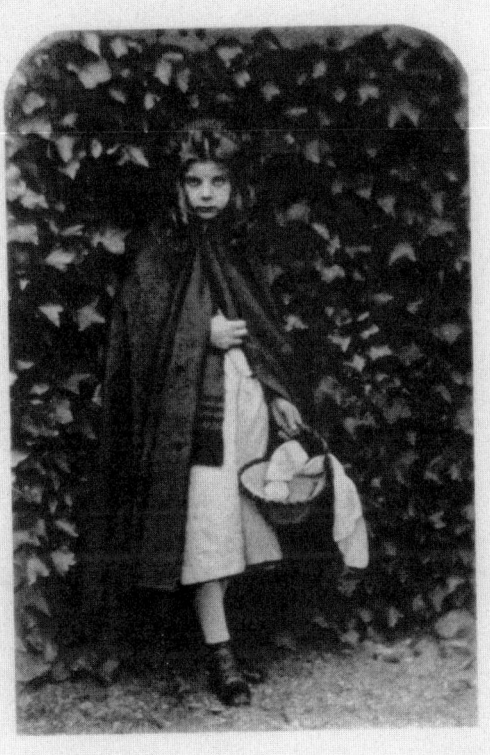

10. AGNES GRACE WELD as "Little Red Riding-Hood"

midnight
cloud
my white with lemon filling heart-shaped cake was eaten.

As the others sang I retreated into my mind to conjure the perfect wish for the moment ahead when I was expected to
white
exhale on the flames. I did not hear them finish their tune. Red and I were on the wing soaring by the warmth of an updraft headed a roundabout to the moon.

"Blow," a voice insisted.

All eleven candles smoked and smelled terrible. I anxiously waited as my mother took the stinky wax out of the cake.
cream
Plucking the last candle from the whipped cream icing, she held it up and teased me about the eleventh being one to grow on, as if to remind me that I was only ten. I was going to grow perfectly well with the help of my new best friend. I never realized the brightness of the moon until Red taught me how to see it.

I had a stomach ache from eating each ribbon tied in a
sunny
bow and every little violet in the frosting nosegay that topped the cake. My mother suggested that a visit to the toilet might be helpful judging from the gas my anus was releasing. I peed party
pee
punch and farted but could not poop. I did not want to let it out. It felt good to be full and pressurized. I intended to hold it in at least until morning so that I might be more inclined to dream all
yellow
night. Lavender soap washed my face and hands. My bed welcomed me and my new friend for our first night together. Even then I hated to sleep alone.

Red seemed at home. My room had walls covered with
lemon
blonde
barn red simulated wood grain paneling. The carpet was a cloud
gold
of white deep pile shag raked to keep it clean and fluffy. Above
gilded
us the ceiling loomed a dark internal fleshy pink. It felt safe and comforting. The shrill noise of the windows reminded me that the bitter cold of February was outside as it whistled and scraped the glass. The bed was small but did not seem that way since I was not very large. Several pillows

propped my head; others waited on the
floor to catch me in case of a fall. Under the
rose chenille bedspread I lay between soft

flames

sheets of midnight blue with a print of the

poop

milkyway splashed across, around, and underneath my
little body. The word KISS was written out on the wall
across from the bed in discs of aluminum foil to mimic
the light bulb sign the band used in their most recent tour. The
silver reflected the glow of the display panel on the stereo left

fleshy

on all night.

From the drawer in my bedside table I grabbed a flash-
light. Red and I retreated under the sheets with our own private
star to light the way as I opened her tiny book. The gold letters

heart

sparkled in the sun. My tummy was barely feeling better as I
relaxed into bed. Red was lying right beside me; I rolled over to
pull her onto my chest and pushed her down gently into my
belly. My thighs were up with my knees folded in toward her
back. I pinched her as hard as I could between my upper thigh
and chest. She had uttered a word before. Perhaps it was the only
word she knew but I intended to make her say it again. And louder this time because I wanted her to admit to me that she was
alive in there and felt just as I did.

"Ow!" She said it again, all right.

Louder too, a lot louder and the voice did not come from
her mouth. The sound of her cry bellowed out from under her
skirt. The sound muffled a bit as the hem of her dress was sand-
wiched between my legs. I noticed that her feet felt large and
awkward though I had presumed them to be as dainty as those
of Cinderella or a dancing princess. The skirt growled again and
I released her. Looking at her angelic face with wide blue
sleeping pools, I reached my hand under her skirt. The
doll was wet. With my eyes closed I pulled her up to my

face and stuck my nose into her wet spot. It smelled like English

rose lavender. I remembered then setting her beside the sink as I washed before bed.

"We smell alike, too!" I said referring to our other similarities.

barn My eyes are blue and my hair is blonde. She was a doll and I wanted to be one. She came from storybookland and I was

cardinal intent on sharing in her adventures. Red was to be my first philosophy.

The phone rang. After two or three chimes I heard my Mother answer. An extension was in my room: a standard upright

blood dial in ox blood. I was relieved when the ringing ceased in my ear. The radio announced a song for lovers as I stooped to open my eyes for a look at the hugeness beneath Red's dress. I could feel that in fact there were no feet at all! As I positioned the light the wolf howled at the moon.

And I saw it. We were eye to eye, his nose protruding out to meet mine. I felt the wind of his throat whistle in my lips as his teeth grabbed the lower part. Moist and warm his voice was gentle. He bit me hard with a snout full of carnivorous teeth. As I cried I felt that my lips were free to move and speak, but I only indulged in breath passing over the site of the initial bite. I could not think of a word. I could only wonder what lips his teeth were holding. I pushed his nose back to my anus and rubbed his stiff whiskers into the aperture already so stressed. A secret garden seemed to swell with life inside of me; I could have died. The next instant his nose was in my face; tongue panting and jowls drooling. I pulled him hard against me as he unlocked that door. A smooth slippery tongue-like key entered the chamber. As it turned, I thought for sure my parents would hear the lock tumble. If not, at least the sound of my head thumping the headboard through the satin-cased rows

50

of goose down. The bass end of the tunes
on the radio helped to shroud my mechanical movement. I felt soggy and steaming;
this fluid state made stasis impossible.
Dominance inspired by pleasure; I crawled on top and
let out a hearty pee. His stuff absorbed my stench and he
was marked as mine for all time.

The moon was erased as the sun pushed its way through cherry
the lace curtains dangling in my window. Upon waking, I realized that I was lying on Red. Under her gown was the form of
another figure. I recognized him as the fearsome wolf from her
story. Flipping the night cap over the large snout, I noticed the
surface of his nose was shiny and sticky with perfume. I turned
the dress over to find those decadent blood swells and sublime reddest
glaciers that charmed me so the day before. There is no absolute
limitation to this relationship with Red.

The phone rang and I stared at it until it stopped. After
a moment my Mother told me to pick up the receiver.

"Don't you just love her?" Aunt Eugenie asked, but I had
no idea how to respond.

"Yes, thank you," I replied.

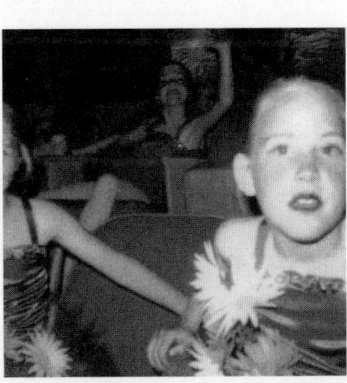

lips

red...
violet

Electr●nic Bar●que:
Notes on Animation **and** Metamorphosis

| *by norman m. klein*

Ours is unquestionably not a postmodern era. I would **prefer to call it electronic baroque, filled with trompe l'oeil** effects, panoramic settings in immersive spaces. And most of all, with odd special-effects "pauses". In the seventeenth century, Bernini wrote that "art consists in everything being simulated although seeming to be real."[1] The viewer pauses as the contrast between simulation and the real merge, then separate, perhaps where the fresco on the wall resembles the stonework framing the dome. For an instant, two media play off each other, a "melange des genres", as French designers called it in the eighteenth century.

The Baroque must be seen as a mutating tradition feeding directly into the nineteenth century through vaudeville, architecture, and particularly animation. We need to understand how the simulation of pauses operates, locate new points of origin, new vocabulary in order to find an epistemic center.

Strings of a Marionette

A chalk line transforms into a man's whiskered face. A hand reaches across the drawing, then erases and redraws the face, aging it, changing its sex, its race. Caricatures of blacks, of Jews, of women's naked thighs appear and dissolve, what was called "lightening hand," at the beginning of the twentieth century.[2] In 1907, Stuart Blackton filmed his lightening hand sketches,[3] as did Winsor McCay four years later.[4] The memory of lightening hand reappears in Otto Messmer's Felix the Cat cartoons of the twenties. Even as late as the forties, Ward Kimble and other Disney animators perform lightening hand as a racy burlesque for soldiers, where the line drawing turns into a naked woman.[5]

Along with chalk[6]— or ink— any number of substances have been used as lightening hand: finger paint on glass; shifting sand; or simply algorithms. But the effect is essentially the same, in hundreds of animated shorts. One medium transmutes into another, from line to protoplasm and back again. The effect on the audience reminds me of animated mercury: a metal that is silvery but flows like liquid — as in f/x films of course, the "morphing" effect initiated with The Abyss, and made standard after Terminator 2.

But this mercury effect varies enormously. In the cartoon, it does not flow in a single stream. It fractures more than flows, in a space that is highly unstable — an architecture of disunities. And yet, the sum is highly structured chaos, very condensed, brilliantly finessed. In my survey of cartoons, Seven Minutes (1993), I use the term "controlled anarchy,"[7] and slip in three pages on metamorphosis,[8] under the rubric of gag. But that is not my subject here.

I have spent the past three years watching the world explode in every special effects film, experimen-

1. Robert T. Petersson, The Art of Ecstacy: Teresa, Bernini, and Cranshaw (New York: Atheneum, 1970), p. 48. **2.** Also called "quick sketches." Film historian Donald Crafton initiated much of the the academic study of lightening hand. He expanded his articles on the subject in Before Mickey: The Animated Film, 1898-1928 (Cambridge, Mass.: MIT Press, 1982). The term "lightening drawing" has become fairly standard in critiques of student work at various film schools (at USC and CalArts certainly). In other words, the problems suggested by linear metamorphosis remain fundamental to the field, even today, with the daunting presence of the computer. **3.** Humorous Phases of Funny Faces, 1906 (Blackton). **4.** Little Nemo, 1911 (McCay). See: John Canemaker, Winsor McCay, His Life and Art (New York: Abbeville Press, 1987), p. 132. Little Nemo was produced by Vitascope, Blackton's company. **5.** Interview with Ward Kimble, July, 1987. **6.** Chalk remains a useful metaphor here, at least as an excuse to play with the material further, add a few terms: Chalk can be erased, broken into dust, be shaded by hand. It has texture, facture, sound, what can be called the haptic (tactile, sinaesthetic). The haptic is essential for all ani-morphed line, for all special effects, in one of two categories: either it looks anabolic (turning food into tissue) or metasomatic (rocks changing substance). The ani-morph should emphasize one of those two as well, to reveal the mode of production (the animator at work), more than the story. For example, chalk is metasomatic, but primordial ooze is anabolic (micro-organisms in mud). The metallic liquid man in Terminator 2 remains fiercely metasomatic. The Brundlefly in The Fly is hopelessly divided, both anabolic and metasomatic. **7.** Klein, Norman M., Seven Minutes: The Life and Death of the American Animated Cartoon (London: Verso, 1993), pp. 41-46, and applied throughout. **8.** Ibid., pp. 64-67.

tal short, and computer game I could find — many I wish I had never seen — while researching my next project, on the history of special effects environments.

From that warped point of view, metamorphosis becomes far more lyrical than a pyramiding of gags. A very different effect is at play. So I need to set up new terms to clarify this difference by examining metamorphosis in animation frame by frame. And finally, a look at what these terms suggest about our political culture at large.

First of all, let me separate the verb from the noun, and shorten "animated metamorphosis" to "ani-morphing".[9] At least that begins to isolate some of the variables.

Ani-morphing can be defined as an animated cycle where metamorphosis takes place. The object appears to change its substance, often very quickly, in two seconds or less, simplified into twenty drawings perhaps.

Let us imagine a mid-point in this cycle, between the extremes, while metamorphosis takes place. Near midway, there is a "lapse", or "hesitation" (terms animators have used). I will call it an "ani-morph". For a few frames, the object — the body, the wall — does not look like what it was, nor what it will be. The ani-morph is the hint of a mess that is revealing. It cracks open a door into the production itself, to the animation studio. Like lightening hand, it reveals how the special effect was assembled, the chalk (sand, paint, or ink) that the animator used.

The ani-morph is literally between the rest of the cycle. The audience catches a glimpse of how animation is made, like noticing the string of a marionette during a show. In modernist terms, the string is a self-reflexive device. It highlights the craft of the animator, not unlike "gesture" in modern painting. Oskar Fischinger's abstract films are

essentially ani-morphs as sensory rhythm.
In animation then, unlike live action film as
a rule, this ani-morph can be extended
almost indefinitely.

These two terms will take my
analysis a long way: the verb "ani-morphing"; the noun "ani-morph". But not

9. I realize that ani-morph is only a letter away from anamorph, and anamorphosis. In future essays, I will explain how close and far away that is.

10. Seven Minutes, pp. 15ff..

far enough. One more noun is needed to make it easier to
describe metamorphosis as a mode of narrative — or what I call
"graphic narrative:"[10] the line drawing put in conflict with the
cinematic space. This hybrid species of story is not simply mythic; it should not be compared to plot points lifted from Ovid's
tales. This is closer to lightening hand than myth; in other words,
closer to illustration and caricature. The animated line always
caricatures another medium; it illustrates, alludes — in the way
Baroque engraving was cut to look like sculpture. It should not
be a faithful copy. It exaggerates as part of the "story" conflict,
hopping from one atmosphere to another. Like a character tip-
toeing on the edge of a roof, the identity of the line must be
unstable, jumping in the viewer's eye from pencil drawing to
forty storeys of glass, down to a pin drop, from painted cel to
movie space.

The drawing not only represents a character on a roof,
as in resemblance, it also "caricatures" the way someone jumps
off. No matter how much like glass and cement the building may
look, the drawing of the character must remain uneasy, hinting
at its origins.

Thus, caricature adds uneasiness in two ways, not simply because it reveals character. It also shows us the animator on
the edge. The drawing is, in "effect", brilliantly corrupt-
ed. Its entendres should catch us by surprise. It is like
Michelangel-esque and Mannerist effects pushed to the

55

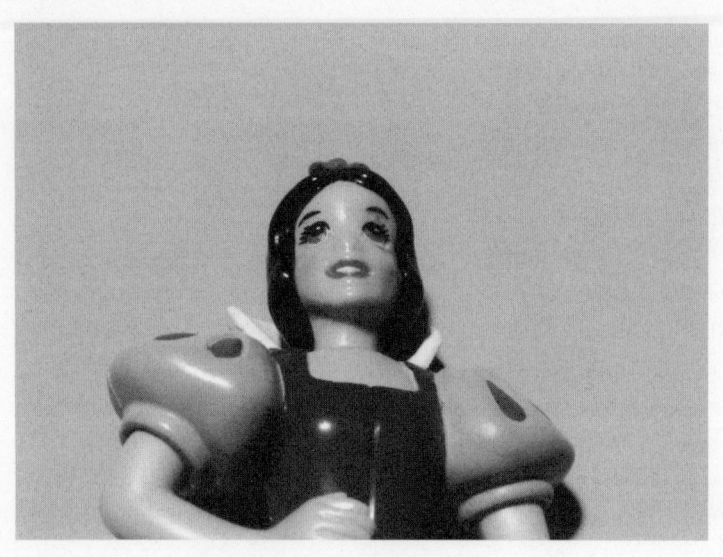

steven hull

limit. When animators take classes in life drawing, they are trained to "see with their eyes," to "forget" the rules of proportion, and instead watch how a body distorts when, for example, the hip turns oddly. The hipbone pressing against the skin should be exaggerated in a Mannerist sense — distressed, to reveal a discomfort, direct the eye of the viewer to where the stress is. The drawing is supposed to resist the act of copying.

But this caricatural effect is only one way to push the limits. Another is to leave part of the drawing empty, not unlike chiaroscuro (but not precisely the same). I am referring here to a species of ani-morph, like Cezanne learning from Japanese woodblock prints, noticing the brilliant omissions. It is chiaroscuro that shows off the cracked black paint hidden behind the three-quarter profile. Omissions are pushed forward slightly, to force the viewer's eye back to the surface. When the effect is done well, the drawing momentarily makes the body appear to dissolve into line, like a sense memory dissolving. The drawing becomes allegorical in Walter Benjamin's sense of allegory — a ruin. It is a version of a phantom. It is shape-shifting that also leaves traces of ink, like a phantom limb, or the shadow of where a picture frame once hung. It presents two story hooks at once: it takes the eye back to the drawing, while it hints at an event that has been forgotten.

The sense that something was erased adds great presence to metamorphosis — the ani-morph reminding us of decay or loss. A temple rubbing is a morphed story. In live-action film grammar, low key lighting is erasure. So when you tell a story on the screen, wherever the "line of the drawing" breaks, there is an ani-morph. I have decided to call the

11. Traced Memory: Clearly, this is a reversal of the term memory traces (the physical trace of the memory in the brain). Here the drawing is misremembered by being traced. For example, in thirties animation, the original drawing was cleaned up, then traced on to another medium: inked and painted on a cel. In the nineties, it is scanned digitally, then paint-boxed. Also, both then and now, the copy or trace can be composited in front of miniatures, or backgrounds.

57

animator's use of erasure "traced memory"[11] (as opposed to memory trace). It is like noticing that a line was made on tracing paper. Very faintly, the viewer realizes that a first drawing was traced somehow. Only the second is left, painted on a cel (that outdated system of animation). Something drawn was taken away in order to make the cel "move" like a movie.[12]

Traced memories go well with Ovid's tales, of course. They fit any myth about metamorphosis, about the ritual journey of discovery, into an underworld. By underworld, I mean a place beneath us, where loss or decay are remembered awkwardly, intimately. Traced memories show the viewer what memory traces feel like in this underworld, because both forms of loss are about shape shifting across dimensions.

Of course, this haunted and self-conscious use of animorphing was not admired universally. Disney, for example, distrusted metamorphosis if it made the animator's drawing too obvious. The revealed scribble weakened the impact of full animation. In the words of Thomas and Johnson, who have become the Boswells of Disney production methods, "when the animator distorts the figure, he must always come back to the original shape."[13] Donald, Pluto or Goofy can be made to bulge and implode, but never lose their "personality," never turn into other "things" in the way Warners' characters did. During the thirties and forties, for example, there are no Disney gag where characters who slam into a wall turn into metal coins, and twirl noisily. That schtick was reserved for MGM Tom and Jerry cartoons.

According to the Disney rule, when a character's body was made of cartoon protoplasm, that stuff was irreducible. Walt was convinced that revealing the drawing while animating flesh could wreck the atmospheric effects that he prized so highly. He preferred wind, water, or heat to test the character's endurance. Nature was at war with the character's body.

Not that Disney did not want his cartoons to show off, quite the contrary. But the tricks he thought would please the crowd made ani-morphs nearly impossible. For example, characters were supposed to trip gracefully, no matter how extreme. Goofy in particular often loses his balance so slowly, he seems at work on a Tai Chi exercise. He rides gravity while it grabs him like a fish hook. No matter how awkward the stretch, his body mass remains amazingly constant. His legs knot up like fishing line, but never lose their mass — never a loose line to remind us of a flat drawing.[14]

By contrast, the Fleischer Studios in the early thirties (1931-33) specialized in ani-morphing, with a simultaneity of effects that is still extraordinary to catalogue; and certainly by Disney standards, seemed to wipe out the "story." Unlike Disney, the Fleischer animators liked to emphasize traced memories when they copied from live movement (rotoscoped). They also used allusion in a more self-reflexive way than at Disney, details drawn from vaudeville theaters and Coney Island rides they knew, as if taking the viewer back to a sketch pad, or to the Coney Island exit off the Brighton Beach line. This strikes me as a useful complement to the traced memory, a kind of allegory of where they went.

Betty Boop's Snow White (1933) is undoubtedly Fleischer's masterpiece, particularly the final sequence in an underworld — both an orphean journey (i.e the myth of Orpheus), and an orphic journey (a silly dance of death set to music). Inside this underworld, ani-morphing governs movement and motivation. For example, the evil queen turns

12. This is similar to what I call "distraction" in The History of Forgetting (London: Verso, 1997).
13. The Illusion of Life, p. 138.
14. See Moving Day (1936), Clock Cleaners (1937), among the best of Art Babbitt's renditions of Goofy. And then the Sport Goofy series directed by Jack Hanna in the forties and fifties.

Koko the Clown into a shapeshifting ghost, while her mirror keeps sprouting hands (an old gag by 1933); the mirror has a rubbery surface that hides a man in blackface.

At the same time, Koko as ghost is rotoscoped from a clip of Cab Calloway. Koko was usually the one who ani-morphed. Of all the Fleischer characters he had been rotoscoped the most often. Graphically, this rotoscoping leaves odd traces, subtle but plain to see. Koko would zap from a cartoon clown who shuffled (buttery head, sack-like body) to a leaner man who ran gracefully (more angles to his chin; a stiffer spinal column). His design helped also, wrapped in cloth, perfect for ghost dancing between bodies, particularly in this, his last extended appearance, his swan song.

Koko sings *Saint James Infirmary*, while turning into a twenty dollar gold piece, then into a "shot of that booze."[15] At the same time, to illustrate the line "crap shootin' pallbearers," the wall behind him is lined with skulls and cows gambling. That bears watching; it is intentionally "traced" like the wall of a Coney Island Mystery Cave Ride. The skulls of African-Americans reenact the greasy underworld of back-alley and saloon life in Harlem. But not Harlem as blacks knew it — this is Harlem as the white male Fleischer animators sensed it. The skulls resemble Currier and Ives prints, with Jim Crow white-on-black pickaninny scowls, and the ooga-booga lips common to American cartoons until the late forties.

The scene is rich enough in allusion to be called a "trace memory", a composite of weekend leisure for the boys at the Fleischer Studios. It is their boozy Manhattan traced in some detail, as an inside joke. On Fridays, the animators used to visit hot spots together, particularly Earl Carroll's Vanities, the Ziegfeld Follies, wrestling, and Hoochie Koochie dance clubs — and of course the Cotton Club, where the

Fleischer Brothers went as well.

Betty's body was a traced composite of women they saw along the way: a garter favored by Hoochie-Koochie dancers;[16] slouching her back like a flapper at a speakeasy; banjo-eyed and bouncy like vaudeville singer Helen Kane; a head like a Coney Island kewpie doll, bobbing on a spring as you shake it.

15. Ani-morphs from this sequence were isolated in Seven Minutes (London: Verso, 1993), for example, p. 79, 93.

The story operates as a metamorphosis, turning a Mystery Cave ride into a blend of Coney Island and Manhattan. After all, Betty/Koko's journey is crammed with versions of shapeshifting, from body to ghost, from frozen death to life — flesh inside out, a world outside caving in. The animation, even the ani-morphs, fit narratively into a very thin musical sketch, as far as story goes. But story can be many things, beyond character and conflict. The ani-morphs (rotoscoping; skeletons and ghosts lapsing) flesh out the absence of plot — a vaudeville tour through the underworld of New York entertainment: cardsharking; running craps on the street; speakeasies in backdoors; boating rides about death in Coney Island. The "story" is about uncertainty; or modernity as the Fleischer team witnessed it. The look was very familiar, at that time.

From 1931 to 1933, Fleischer cartoons have a peculiar bite to them — and not in those years alone, simply greater emphasis during the early sound era. Bimbo's Initiation is another curious example (1931). Bimbo, as if trapped in immigrant panic, is being forced to spin into a labyrinth of imprisoning rooms, some out to stab him, others gulping him, or forcing him to crawl across the ceiling (the comparison with Kafka's Gregor Samsa seems unavoidable, but we must remember that the Fleischers knew nothing of European

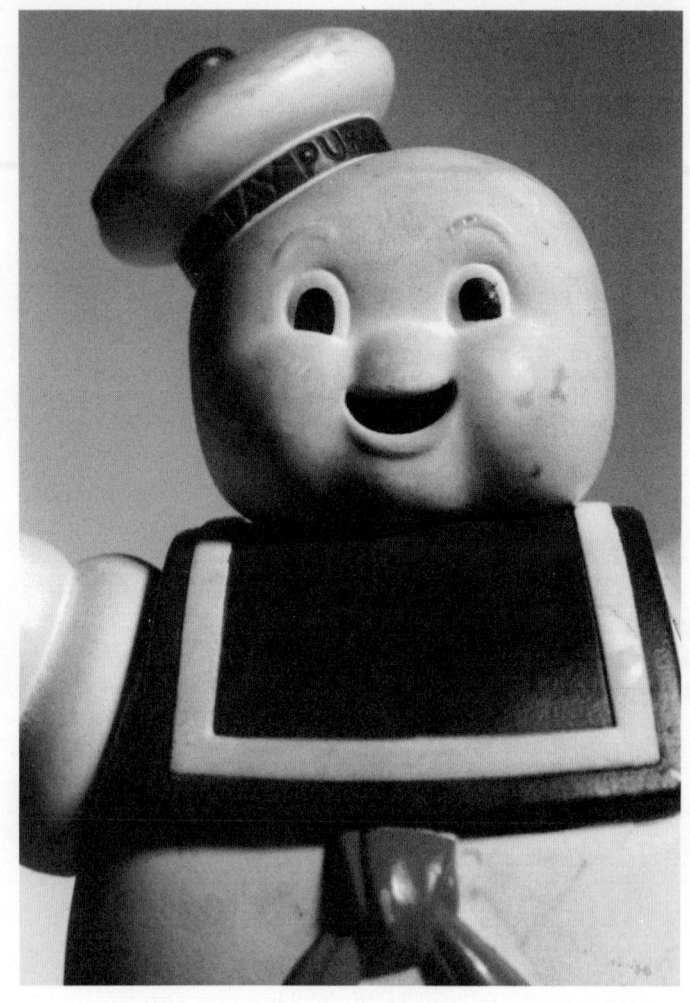

steven hull

modernist literature, or Surrealist theater,
film; theirs was a homegrown pathology of
urban life).

Bimbo keeps refusing to be a "mem-
ber," to what seems like a strange bundist
or masonic order in caricature — men
with spent candles for heads, as if they

16. Hoochie-Koochie: a pseudo Egyptian, belly dance that was popular at burlesques and "Hoochie Koochi" parlors.

inhabited the night where dead candles wind up, the coolness
after the night light goes out. Finally, one of the leaders pulls off
her hood (this in an era that had witnessed a huge revival of the
Ku Klux Klan), and turns out to be the sexiest poodle Bimbo had
ever seen, "a pip" he calls her. She does a bumptuous bump and
grind for him. He grins as if he were being tickled from the inside
out, lasciviously; his eyes follow her — she's an earlier version of
Betty Boop. Then, every one of the hooded KKK bundists take
off their hoods. They're all voluptuous Betty Boops. He slaps her
ass; she slaps his — a raunchy version of black bottom. Then a
gleeful layer-cake chorus-line finale ends the short in the way
most of the Fleischer cartoons of that era ended, like a Victor
recording that runs out of threads and simply stops, with a final
trumpet or downbeat.

This is a dark piece of work for kiddies to watch, even
for adults. And there were others like it from Fleischer, even in
the twenties. In two of the most remembered: the world explodes
and New York goes cockeyed in Koko's Earth Control (1928); or
Max gets multiplied industrially and attacks Koko in Koko's
Cartoon Factory (1925). Later, under the censorship during the
Shirley Temple era in the mid-thirties, their macabre twists look
even more repressed, more about guilt than dancing on your
grave. Two cartoons from 1936, Cobweb Hotel and Small
Fry, have become cult favorites in weird cartoon collections. They each are built around nightmare chases like

the Boop cartoons, but here instead of bouncy dance numbers, we see flies tortured, or baby fish forced to swim through inky inversions like Lethean death.

So while Fleischer employs fewer morphing gags as the thirties goes on, tries to resemble Disney full animation much more, something of the allegory of darkside out remains. I have always assumed that this insistent diabolerie came out of the immigrant world they knew from Bedford-Stuyvesant, Brooklyn as children — the xenophobia of a Jewish childhood, living as part of the largest influx of foreign immigrants to hit any American city (rivaled only by the massive influx into Los Angeles since 1970). In New York then, as in Los Angeles now, up to 25% of the total population were foreign born. It is in itself something of a molten metamorphosis. And it generates bizarre panics, which are heightened by economic disasters like the Great Depression (first of the 1890's, prelude to 1929); or like the class warfare, the strikes, the street fighting. I am reminded, of course, of the shock waves in L.A. from 1992 through 1994 (looting, fires, earthquakes, massive recession). This comparison brings me back to f/x blockbusters again, like Independence Day, part of a bumper crop of disaster movies inspired by the shocks of 1992-94. They bear a faint backhanded similarity to the ani-morphing irony of Fleischer cartoons. Let us say simply an instructive parallel.

Obviously, I prefer Fleischer shorts to the bloated disaster pic, but I still can see many of the same allegories in both "vehicles," about powerlessness, about alien presence, about underworlds where the animator turns urban fear into an amusement park. I imagine the powerbrokers in the film industry (1993-94) watching houses burn in Malibu; or their pool spilling over while everything made of glass explodes during the earthquake. Then, after the shaking subsides, or the fires are put out, they head for a local watering hole in West Hollywood perhaps, and decide to greenlight any film that sounds like a special-effects disaster epic. Somehow, it feels right to turn the route they drive to make power lunches in West Hollywood into traced memories in Escape from New York or Volcano.

While dramatic structure is being hybridized by new effects, this look that comes out warns us, something about identity dissolving under the multiple impact like bodies in lava, or under biblical final judgement inside a tornado. We have to study the specific production methods for metamorphosis, interview animators, effects people, check the details of the promo kit sent out by the studio, try to locate an epistemic center out of all this. The vocabulary will always take us back to mythic tales about decay, traced memories, an uneasy blend of distancing effects and vivid expressionist gimmickry.

But surely, if we are to begin to make this dragon of morphing effects speak less about corporate spectacle, and more about private loss, we also have to study how animation operates frame by frame — the building blocks of our trans-morphology into whatever this new political culture will finally be called. Is it electronic baroque, a very late feudalism, or simply intranational cybernetic double-speak.

I am convinced that new modes of film can be developed out of ani-morphic effects. But they should come from the experimental wing of our culture. What worries me, however, is that they may come from Microsoft or Disney instead. All this effects mastery may be applied merely for the pleasure of global corporate fantasy, for the wall of the new Planet Hollywood.

65

Strange Loops, or
Tangled Hierarchies

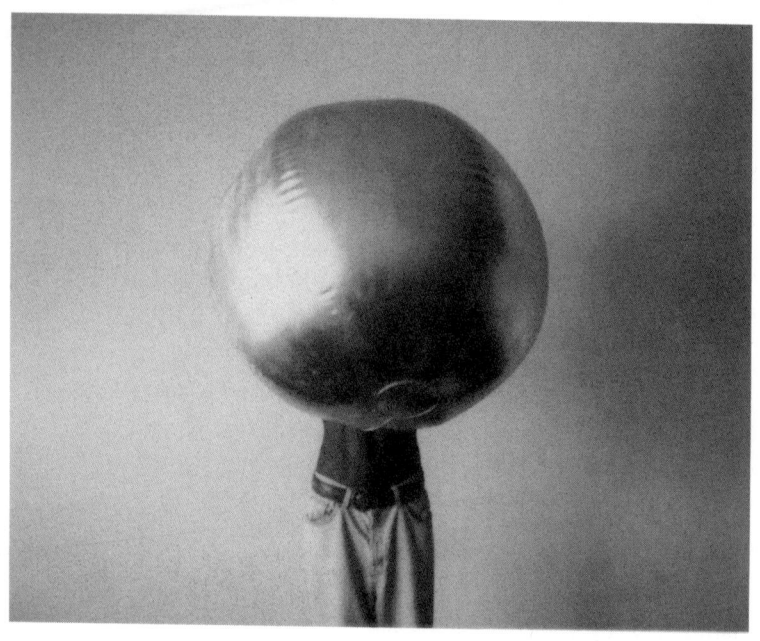

daniel j. martinez

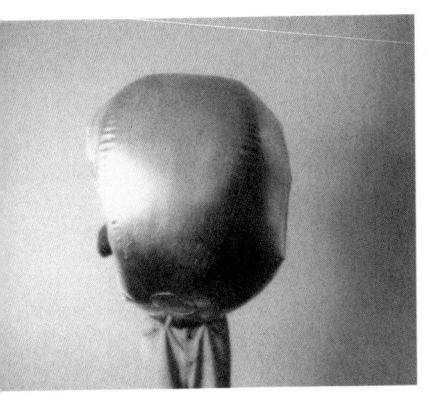 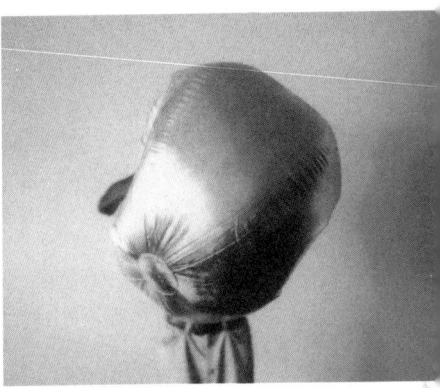

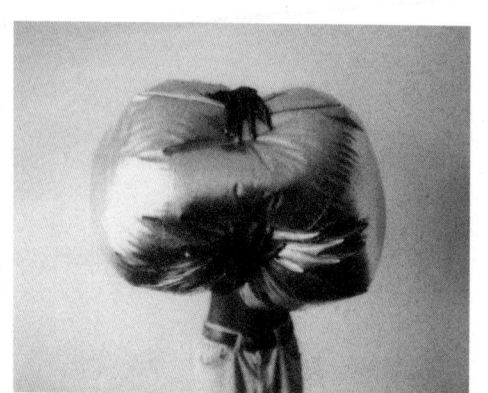

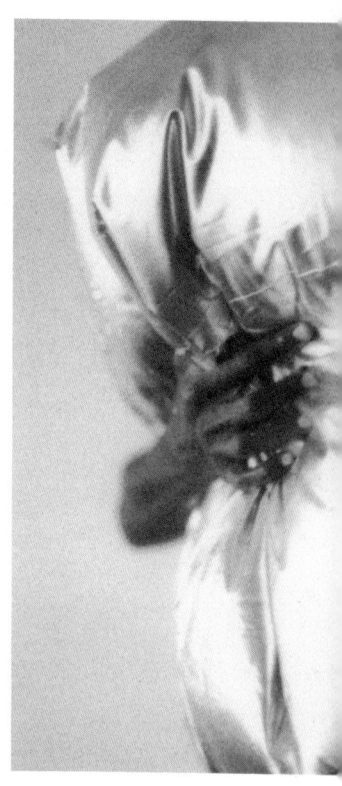

daniel j. martinez

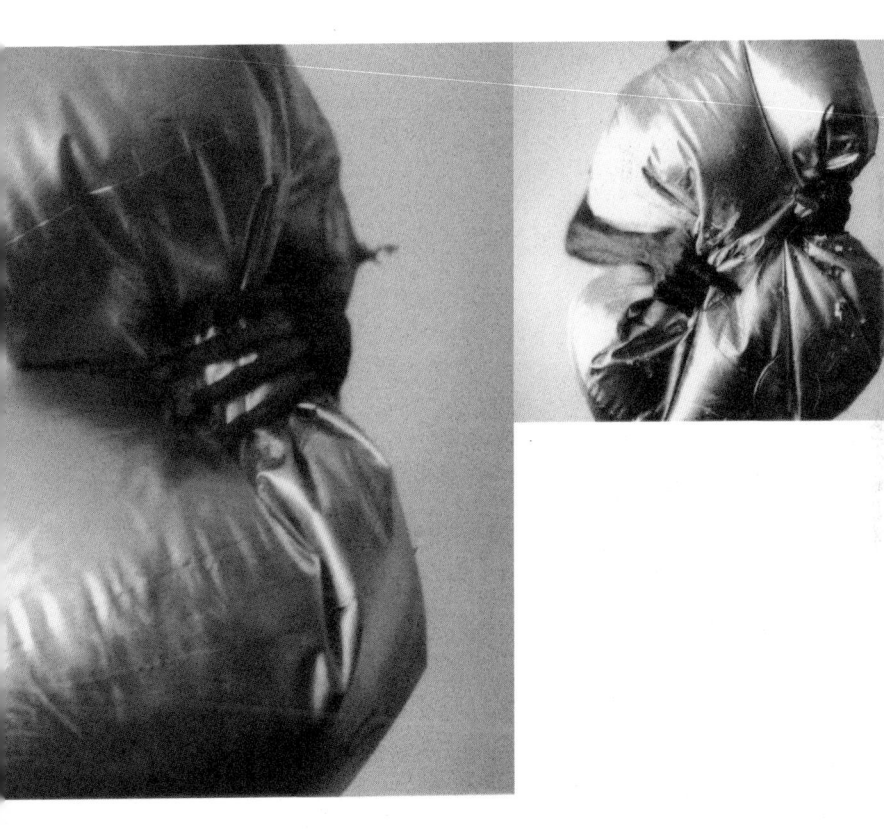

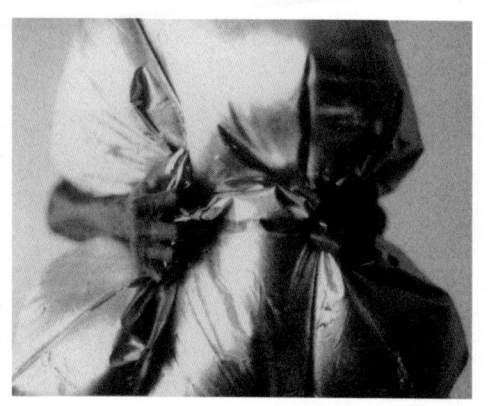

daniel j. martinez

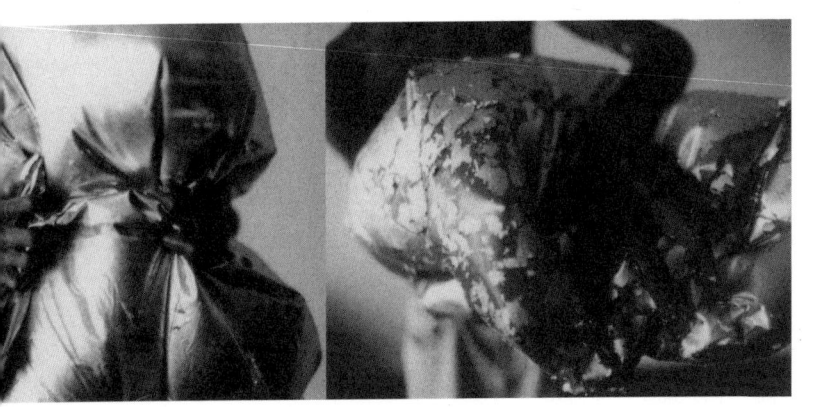

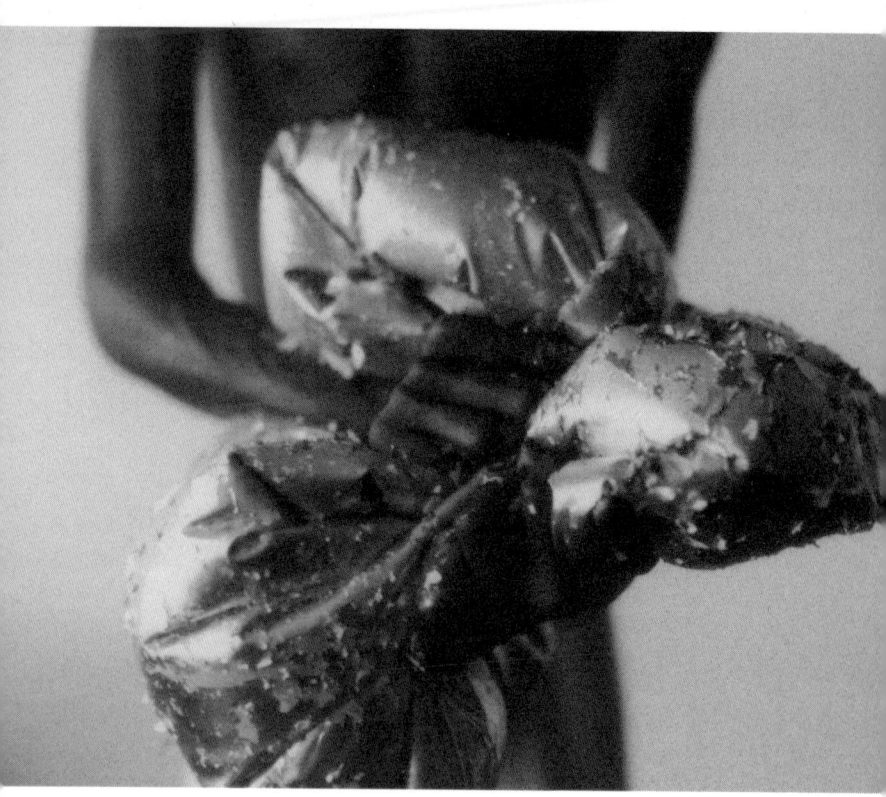

daniel j. martinez

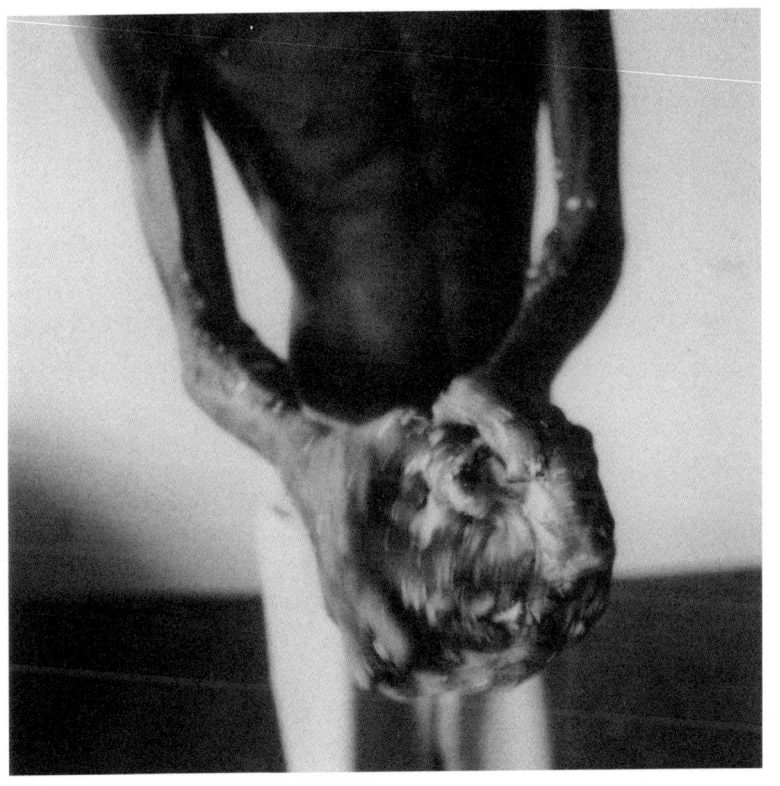

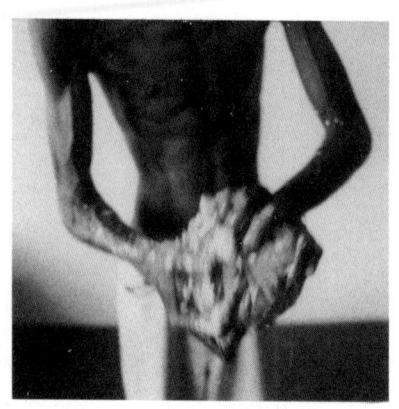

daniel j. martinez

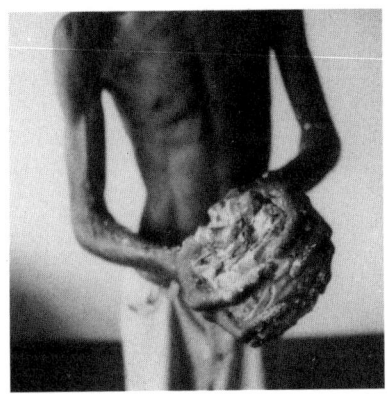

the world is hollow, and I have touched the sky.

s(•)rry

| by liz young

Sorry I crossed the street
when I wasn't supposed to.
Sorry Sandy told on me.
Sorry her parents were never
home. Sorry they were white trash.

Sorry I wouldn't let Mother finish the story. Sorry I couldn't bear to listen. Sorry she can't read to me now.

Sorry I kissed Robert behind the bushes, or was it Dean? Sorry I can't remember the first boy I ever kissed.

Sorry I made Paul pee in
front of me. Sorry I wanted
to see his willy. Sorry it made
me feel strange.

Sorry I was afraid of my
body. Sorry it gave me bad
dreams. Sorry I didn't want
to grow up.

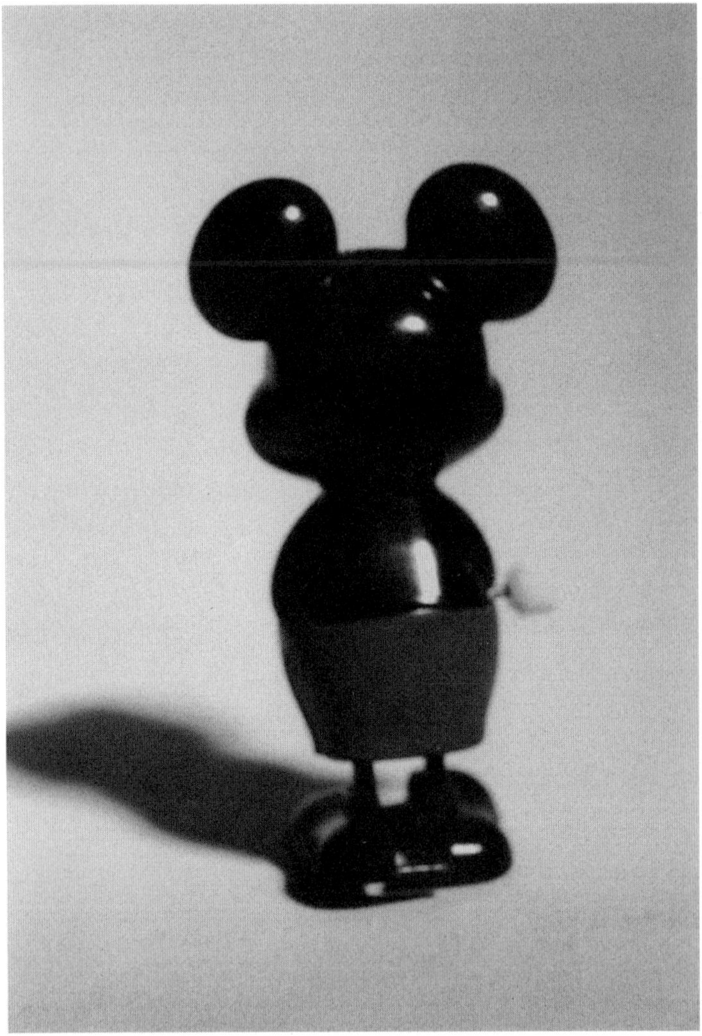

steven hull

80